Table of Contents

This book is dedicated to the Goddess in Her many forms and to her priestesses.

Written and illustrated by Tara L. Reynolds © 2015
loveofthegoddess.blogspot.com

Introduction

This book was written for beginners on the goddess path but anyone at any point of their path can also gain knowledge from this book. My hope with this book is to help people discover and connect with their own goddess. To show people how to connect with their energy through different exercises to take part in. This is a very interactive book and while there is background information about each goddess, that is not the main focus of this book. There are many great books out there on all the goddesses within this book that you can research for yourself and I greatly encourage that. But for this book, the focus is on connecting with these goddesses. Learning how to call on them, pray to them and work with their energies in ritual. This book will help you to build a relationship with your goddess which is a very fulfilling experience.

Certain goddess energies will resonate with you more than others. Each goddess has a different purpose and is comprised of many different attributes. Just like we as people have many different layers to ourselves and our personalities, so do the gods. And not all personality types are right with some people, and it works the same way with working with goddess energy. Some will resonate with you deeply, and some won't. The trick is to find your special goddess or goddesses to work with.

This book contains nine goddesses from five different pantheons including Egyptian, Greek, Celtic, Norse, and Yoruban. Each goddess has a guided meditation and two connection exercises. These are given as a guide to show you ways in which you can honor each goddess. And they can also be used as a guide for when you create your own rituals. In the exercises, the altars you will create and supplies you will use are very basic. Feel free to change or add anything else to your ritual to make it your own. I'm just here to give you the foundation for which you will create your own practice with.

All of my sources are cited at the end of this book and they are organized by goddess. All of the books listed in my sources can also be great books for further reading about any of the goddesses here. Enjoy your journey to discovering and connecting with your goddess! You are on the path of the priestess.

Isis, Egyptian Mother Goddess

Isis, Egyptian Mother Goddess of the Universe, was worshiped and revered all over the ancient world. She is considered the *"Mother of All"* or *"The Goddess of Ten Thousand names"*, representing her feminine power and act of creation. Isis was seen as a Great Mother Goddess, she was also seen as a mistress of magic, rebirth, healing, resurrection, and childbirth. She was very much loved by her people. This is said to be because she was a very compassionate and nurturing Goddess, and was portrayed to be like one of them. To be on their level, one with the people. Her worship was so important; history says that it was hard for the ancients to finally let go of their beloved Isis when Christianity came charging forward.

In the myth of Isis and Osiris, her brother-husband, you can see her undying love shining through in a wonderful and passionate love story. Osiris was killed by Set, who was jealous of Osiris's position as king. He made a wooden sarcophagus to fit Osiris's measurements. At a party, he tricked Osiris to get in the sarcophagus, and then closed and locked it shut. It was then sealed with lead and thrown into the Nile. Upon hearing that Osiris was gone, Isis set out to look for him. She later learned that the coffin had floated down the Nile river. When she found the coffin, she hid it in an area of marshland. Although Set ends up finding the coffin. He opened the coffin and dismembered Osiris into fourteen pieces, scattering them across the land of Egypt. 1

Isis then set out to look for the pieces of her beloved. She found all but one, his penis.
She decided to fashion a phallus out of gold, and sing a song to Osiris until he came back to life. Once Osiris was resurrected, he could then have a proper Egyptian ceremony and burial.
After Isis brought Osiris back to life, she made love to him with the golden phallus. She became pregnant and fled the land to hide from her jealous brother Set. She then gave birth to her son, the falcon headed God Horus.
2

It is easy to see in her myth, how loving and compassionate she was towards her family. She would stop at nothing to protect her loved ones. Very much like a Mother and her child. Which is why she was seen as a strong Mother Goddess. Her passion and courage in her myths is powerful and admirable. Isis was also the *Great Healer* or the *Great Physician*. It is well known that there were many healing rites where people called on Isis for her great healing abilities. Many times for these healing rituals, dream incubation was used. People would stay at the temple and follow a very precise daily regimen prescribed by the Priests, and then the person would sleep in the temple hoping to receive guidance from Isis through their dreams. The Priests and Priestesses of the temple of Isis were also said to be physicians, or skilled in the healing arts. Everything ranging from knowledge of human anatomy, producing medicines, knowledge of common and rare diseases, and surgical techniques, among many others. 3

One of the temples of Isis was called *The Temple of Isis Medica*, which was in *Menouthis,* a sacred city in ancient Egypt devoted to the Goddess Isis. Her ability to heal the sick was well known throughout the ancient world. 4 She was also seen as Patroness of traveling by ship, or travel in general. The Nile was seen as the life force in ancient Egypt. Their whole world depended on the life sustaining powers of the Nile. So of course Isis would be associated with this essential part of Egyptian life. She was called *Isis Pelagia*, or *Isis of the Sea* and she was the Goddess whose tears filled the Nile every year. 5

In Alexandria she was honored at the shore to grant good fortune for those about to embark on their journeys, or for those coming home. She was honored every year at a celebration known as *The Ploiaphaesia*, or the *Festival of Navigation*. At this festival people would send out "*The Ships of Isis*" which were boats filled with offerings of incense, flowers, libations and small shrines. 6 The ancient Egyptians were known for their many festivals throughout the year and many were dedicated to Isis. Isis was honored at every full moon known as the "Fifteenth Day Feast" which fell on the 15th day of the ancient Egyptian Lunar calendar. This full moon feast was held in honor of Isis and Osiris, which usually consisted of foods that were white in color and were either round or crescent shaped. These foods could be cakes, peeled potatoes, white rice, cheese and milk. 7

Night of the Teardrop or *Feast of the Waters of the Nile,* was a festival for Isis which honors Isis and her sorrows as she weeps for Osiris, and her tears flood the Nile. The exact dates of many Egyptian festivals are not really known but it is thought that this festival happened sometime between June and July. 8 Another festival thought to have taken place in the fall was *The Isia,* a six-day festival, celebrating Isis's search for Osiris. On the last day of the festival, Osiris's rebirth is celebrated. 9

Being that Isis was worshiped all throughout the ancient world, she became associated with many of the Greek and Roman Goddesses, and also had temples in these other lands. She was honored in Greece, as a kind of trio of Goddesses, Artemis, Isis and Hekate. 10 In Rome she was equated with the Goddess Diana. 11 It is said that the image of the Virgin Mary nursing Jesus was taken from the images of Isis nursing her son Horus. She was also associated with the Egyptian Cat Goddess Bast, since cats were sacred to Isis. 12

Isis was honored all over the ancient world, and it was quite a battle for the Christians to try and take away Isis from her deeply devoted followers. She is an all loving and all-knowing Goddess. She is the Universe itself and the creator of life, love and compassion. Isis can be invoked for many different things. Her powers stretch far and wide. In the following pages you will do exercises and a guided meditation to help you connect with this Mother Goddess of the Universe.

Goddess Connections

Isis teaches us to be loving and compassionate towards others. To protect and nurture our family, and ourselves. She helps us to love ourselves, and shows us that the universal healing energy is, love. She helps us to heal from within and nurture our souls. She teaches us how to create our dreams and achieve our goals. She also shows us that the love of a mother can be strong and powerful. Isis would be a great Goddess for those women approaching motherhood. Call on her to learn to love yourself and others. To be compassionate towards all human beings, and respective of their own path's, and to protect you and your family.

Guided Meditation to Meet Isis

Guided meditation is an essential part of connecting with your Goddess. Not only does it relax your body, it also prepares your mind to connect to her energy. In this exercise, you will take a journey to meet Isis, and ask her for guidance for any issues that are troubling you.

Before any meditation make sure to ground and center yourself. Take some slow and deep breaths in and out a few times until you feel relaxed. You may also want to burn a smudge stick to cleanse the area. Once you feel centered you may start the meditation.

Imagine you are walking through a forest. You notice that you are approaching a lake, there is a small boat parked there with a woman standing on the dock. She asks you if you would like a ride. You say yes and get on the boat. Slowly the boat takes off up stream. It's a beautiful day, you close your eyes and feel the warm breeze on your face. When you open your eyes you are no longer on the lake, you are now going up the Nile river, with palms and papyrus along the shore blowing against the breeze, and the smell of incense in the air. You notice your boat driver, is now wearing a flowing long white dress, with gold jewelry and dark kohl around her eyes. She winks and smiles at you. She stops the boat at a dock, and you get off with her. Right before you is a huge temple. With people bustling all about. Women carrying bowls of fruit and herbs. You smell incense and perfumed unguents on the people passing you by.

The woman you are with tells you " Today is a celebration for Isis" she invites you to join her in the temple. You follow her and the other women who are all wearing the same white dresses and gold jewelry, they go into the temple. Once inside there stands before you a beautiful statue of Isis. All the women bow down at her feet and leave offerings of flowers, figs and resins. You realize that these women are priestesses of Isis. It's your turn to bow at the Great Goddess. When you rise back up, you notice that the statue is no longer a statue at all, but a beautiful woman, with long dark hair, kohl around her eyes and covered in jewelry of lapis lazuli and gold. Your breath escapes you as you realize, she is Isis. She looks at you and smiles. She then unfolds her great golden wings and wraps them around you. Imagine white and golden light emanating from the goddess, flowing from her wings and body and going through your whole body. Feel her motherly love and protection. Hold this image and feeling for a few minutes. Now the goddess releases you after a long embrace, and she asks you what you need her guidance for. Tell her what's troubling you and listen for her answer. She may speak it or show you a symbol, just make sure to pay attention to any messages she may give you, and hold this image for a little while.

Now thank Isis and embrace her once more. You glance around and notice that you are now alone in the temple, except for the guide who lead you there standing by the door. You look back to Isis and notice that she is no longer there, but the statue you first saw is. You walk back to your guide and follow her back out to the boat. She takes you back down the Nile, back to the forest you originally were. Take a few deep breaths to come back. Once you feel ready, open your eyes and ground yourself. Take a few cleansing breaths, and make sure to thank Isis for her guidance.

Write down your experience in your journal. Your answer may not come to you right away, but soon enough it will reveal itself to you. If you feel the need, practice this meditation a few times until you get a more concrete answer.

Full Moon Ritual to Create your Dreams with Isis

Isis is a goddess of fertility and creation and has the ability to help you transform your life by creating your desires, dreams and goals. Whether it be a business venture, creative endeavor or any other goals you have set for yourself, Isis can help you create it. This ritual is meant to be performed on the full moon. So that the moon is at it's full power to help you get what you desire.

Supplies:
Candle
Sage bundle
Sandalwood incense
Piece of paper
Fireproof dish/cauldron
Offering (resins/herbs)

Write on your piece of paper what it is your trying to create, for example: *A successful business.* Set up your altar, light your sage bundle and cleanse yourself and your area with the smoke. Light your candle and incense and recite:

Isis, Great Mother Goddess of creation and transformation,
lend me your power so that I may create (insert goal/dream here)
and achieve my life's goals and dreams.

Now burn your paper with your goal written on it in the flame of the candle, and throw it into the fire proof dish. Watch the smoke as it rises sending your wish out into the universe. Visualize your dream coming true, imagine yourself already living it and have accomplished your goal. Meditate for a few minutes, then take a few deep breaths and thank Isis for her help. Leave a small offering for Isis. Record the whole ritual in your journal and any visions that may have come through as well. Also be sure to record your dreams, as sometimes, our goddesses will give us messages while we're in the dream world.

Isis Healing Dream Ritual

Known for her healing qualities, Isis can help you to heal spiritually and mentally. Whether it be the loss of something dear to you like a friendship, or if you need to heal within to forgive another, or you just want to rejuvenate your soul with the warm healing embrace of Isis, any hurtful situation you experience you may call on Isis to heal you. Of course for physical ailments please consult your doctor.

This will be a night-time ritual before bed and to be performed on the waxing moon so that as the moon grows, so does your healing. Start this night-time ritual off by taking a relaxing bath with a few drops of lavender essential oil. A great way to prepare for internal healing is to cleanse your body as well as this will prepare your mind for purification and ritual.

Supplies:
Lavender essential oil
Sage bundle
Myrrh resin
Charcoal disc
Fireproof bowl/ incense holder
Offering of rose petals
Journal and pen to record dream

After you've taken your cleansing bath, go to your bedroom, and burn your myrrh resin next to your bed. Make sure your bed is set up comfortably. Turn off the lights like you are preparing for sleep. Lay down and make sure your comfortable. Now recite:

Isis, Great Mother Goddess of healing and love,
I invoke your presence on this night as the moon grows,
Help me to heal myself from(insert problem)
So I can achieve balance and move on with my life,
Embrace me with your wings of gold
And help me to heal from this problem I've told,
Reveal in my dreams your secrets to heal,
Lady of magic, change the way I feel.

Now thank Isis and add more myrrh resin to your charcoal block if needed. Fall asleep while smelling the sacred scent. You might not fall asleep right away and it's okay to move around if you're not comfortable. In the morning record your dreams and see if there's any messages from Isis.

Hathor, Egyptian Cow Goddess

13

Hathor is the Egyptian goddess of love, dance, happiness, sexuality and women. Her name in Egyptian is spelled Hwt-hwr which means "House of Horus". This refers to Horus the elder who is the falcon god not the son of Isis and Osiris. 1 Hathor is a very ancient goddess and her main cult site of worship was at Dendera. Evidence of her worship has also been found in Thebes, Luxor and a shrine was found at Deir el-Bahri .2

Hathor has many faces and different aspects. She has been portrayed as a cow goddess with the face of a woman and the ears of a cow. In ancient Egypt the cow was seen as a sacred animal which represented rebirth and the cycles of life. Women and cows were spiritually connected because of their sacred milk and life giving powers.3 Hathor in her cow goddess form is said to stem from the primeval cow goddesses of Neolithic worshipers. Over time these ancient deities which were originally associated with the animals, the land and the sky were transformed into the more modern deities with human-like qualities. 4

Hathor is also a sun and sky goddess who is referred to as "The Golden One". She wears the sun disc crown and the serpent uraeus as her headdress. 5 She is associated with dawn and the rising sun as this is a time of renewal and new beginnings. It is said that her father Ra crosses the sky each day because of his love for her and that without her help there would be no sunrise. 6

Carved onto the columns of many of her temples throughout Egypt there are what's known as "Hathor heads". These were on the top of the columns and they were just the head of Hathor in her cow goddess depiction. 7 Since she is associated with the cow this means that she is also a goddess of fertility and childbirth. A mother goddess in her own right.

Hathor is daughter to the god Ra, the sun god and Nut, the sky goddess. In some stories though she is portrayed as the Mother of Ra or the Partner of Ra. 8 Hathor also has a great association with the lioness goddess Sekhmet and the two are sometimes so entwined in myth that it seems as though they are aspects of one goddess. In her Sekhmet persona she is known as the "Eye of Ra". 9 One such tale describing Hathor in her Sekhmet guise is the myth of the destruction of humanity.

People were plotting to rebel against Ra so he decided to destroy mankind and start over again. He sent down his eye in the form of Sekhmet to fight against the rebels. He then decided to call all the gods together so they could discuss what should be done. They decide that he should call back Sekhmet and send his eye down again as Hathor to bring about peace. When Ra calls his eye back to him though, the goddess refuses and says that she has dominated mankind and is enjoying it. Ra quickly devises a plan to trick Sekhmet. He orders 7,000 jars of beer to be colored red and to be poured onto the fields. When Sekhmet sees this she thinks it's blood and drinks all of it. Now in her drunkenness she returns to Ra having forgotten about mankind. To celebrate their survival, Ra orders mankind to have an annual festival with intoxicating drinks in honor of the goddess. 10 This is where she gets her epithet "Lady of Drunkenness" from.

Hathor was also the "Mistress of Dance" and the "Mistress of Music". Music and dance were a central aspect of ritual in the Egyptian world. It is thought that music and dance were used as a way to induce trance during rituals and celebrations. Sacred dance was seen as a way to honor Hathor and pay her homage. 11 During the dances the women would play the sistrum which was like a rattle. The sistrum is a sacred instrument of Hathor and was often decorated with a Hathor head. Some of the sacred dances were known to also be acrobatic displays. 12 There was also dancing for funerary rites in which invocations to Hathor were made. 13 During certain festivals such as "The Festival of Drunkenness" the king would dance in front of Hathor as a way to appease her. 14

While we can't be certain of what exactly the music sounded like during these rituals, we do know some of the instruments that were used. Some of the most popular seem to have been the sistrum, tambourine, lyre, harp, clapper and the drum. 15 Song was also an integral part of the music played during these rituals. There are songs inscribed on the walls of the

15

temples which invoke Hathor. It seems as though many of the musicians were priestesses and the singers were female too. The position of temple singer was a very prestigious one and women favored these positions. 16

Hathor was also a goddess of love and sexuality. She was said to bring lovers together and to reignite passion between lovers who were in long term relationships. She was prayed to for success in marriages. 17 Hathor was also associated with perfumes and fragrance. Incense was very common in ancient Egypt and it was burned in all the temples. The ancient Egyptians themselves were known for their sweet smelling perfumes. Flowers, perfumes and incense were all given as offerings to the goddess of love as scent was seen as sacred and perfume was seen as a gift from the gods. 18 In the temples of Hathor at Dendera there were workshops where sacred perfumes, incense and unguents were made. The recipes and ingredients were inscribed on the walls of the temples. The most famous recipe and well known even today is Kyphi. 19

In the following pages you will do exercises and a guided meditation to help you connect with this Mistress of Music and Dance.

Goddess Connections

Hathor represents the mother figure. She teaches us to not only be a mother to others but to also mother ourselves. Hathor helps us to indulge in life and ritual. She teaches us that dance and music are the way to lighten yourself with playfulness. Hathor also represents love and passion and she helps us to keep our relationships alive. She also teaches us to be passionate in our endeavours. Hathor is the rising sun and she shows us that each day is a new opportunity and a new beginning.

Guided Meditation to Meet Hathor

Guided meditation is an essential part of connecting with your Goddess. Not only does it relax your body, it also prepares your mind to connect to her energy. In this exercise, you will take a journey to meet Hathor, and ask her for guidance for any issues that are troubling you.

Before any meditation make sure to ground and center yourself. Take some slow and deep breaths in and out a few times until you feel relaxed. You may also want to burn a smudge stick to cleanse the area. Once you feel centered you may begin the meditation.

Imagine that you are walking through tall grasses and there is a body of water beside you. This is the Nile River. It's morning just at sunrise. You notice the top of the sun peaking over the horizon and you decide to sit and watch it rise. There's a cool breeze coming off the river and you close your eyes to feel it better. When you open them, there is a beautiful woman standing before you in the sunrise. The sun becomes her headdress and it shines brightly on the top of her head. She smiles at you and you realize that this is the goddess Hathor.

You stand up and greet her. She embraces you in a motherly hug. She stands with you and together you finish watching the sun rise. She then takes your hand and you walk along the edge of the Nile together. At this point you may want to ask her for any guidance or ask her if she has any messages for you. Listen to what she says and take it all in.

You are approaching the end of your walk and you notice that you're coming upon a large temple. This temple has columns with Hathor heads in her cow goddess form. As you get closer you hear beautiful music emanating from inside. The music calls to you. It calls to your body and you feel yourself slowly start to sway with the rhythm. Hathor invites you inside the temple to take part in the temple dances in her honor.

Once inside you notice that there is lots of sweet smelling incense smoke which creates a hazy magical feel to the temple. There are women dancing and playing instruments such as the sistrum and the tambourine. There are even women doing a form of acrobatics. They seem to be in a trance from all the dancing and music. You look to Hathor who hands you a sistrum and instructs you to start dancing with the rest of the women. She takes her place as well and slowly starts to dance as she shakes her sistrum. You follow her lead.

You start to move your hips with the rhythm of the sounds coming from the sistrum. You become immersed in the dance and lose yourself in the ecstatic energy. You dance and dance and shake your sistrum until you are in the same rhythm with the rest of the women. You eventually enter into a trance and go deeply into your own world forgetting the scene around you. Dance for a little while so you can fully feel the energy.

You keep dancing until slowly you start to come out of your trance. You notice that the women who were dancing are no longer there. The temple is empty except for a beautiful, large statue of Hathor in its center. You walk up to the statue and you notice that she has a sly smile on her face. There are some flowers to your right that are left there for people to leave offerings. You pick some up, place them at her feet and thank her for a wonderful experience.

As you are leaving the temple, you turn back around one more time to glance at the statue of Hathor. She is smiling at you and you feel as though you may have saw her wink at you. Now you exit the temple and walk back towards the Nile River. Walk back through the tall grasses to where you originally started. Take a few deep breaths to come back. Once you feel ready, open your eyes and ground yourself. Take a few cleansing breaths, and thank Hathor for her guidance.

Write down your experience in your journal. Your answer may not come to you right away, but soon enough it will reveal itself to you. If you feel the need, practice this meditation a few times until you get a more concrete answer.

Sunrise Ritual to Hathor

Since Hathor is a solar goddess associated with the sun, performing a sunrise ritual would be a great way to honor her. Find somewhere in nature where you can safely go to watch the sunrise. It can be a beach, mountain top, park or even just in your own backyard. Anywhere that you will get a good view of the sunrise. It's important to fully connect with the energy of the sun as it's rising so having a good view of it will make the difference.

You will need to wake up early for this one. The sunrise time can change a little each morning so check the day before and prepare yourself ahead of time. You may wish to smudge yourself with sage before you go or if you're not a morning person (like myself) you may wish to just grab some coffee and head out. Feel free to bring a camera to get some good shots of the sunrise as a way for you to remember your experience. I would also recommend bringing an offering for Hathor. This can be sweet smelling flowers, incense, myrrh resin or some of your favorite perfume. Just remember that you will be leaving this offering outside so make sure it is natural and bio-degradable.

Once you get to your sunrise spot, clear your mind and take a few deep breaths. You will want to arrive a few minutes before the sunrise.

Morning can be such a magical time of day. It's usually quiet and there's sense of tranquility that has a hold over everything. Look around you and take in your surroundings. You will hear the birds singing their morning songs. You may hear crickets chirping and other animals coming to life for the new day. Notice the temperature, if there's a cool breeze or if it's a warm morning. Totally immerse yourself in your surroundings. Once you start to see the sunrise over the horizon, recite the following prayer to Hathor:

Hathor, Lady of Heaven
Golden One
I pray to you as the sun rises
Fill me with your light and warmth
Teach me your ways
I will dance at your altar
I will light your incense
And honor your greatness
Lady of the Sky
I honor you on this sunrise.

After you say your prayer continue to watch the sunrise. Imagine that the glowing sun is the sun disc on Hathor's headdress flanked by bull horns. Imagine that Hathor herself is rising as the sun. Feel the energy of the rising sun filling you with it's promise of a new day. Watch the sunrise until it reaches it's zenith in the sky. Thank Hathor for her beautiful sunrise and leave your offering. After this you may continue on with your day. Be sure to write down your experience in your journal along with any messages that may have come through.

Make a Sistrum with Hathor

A sistrum is a musical instrument similar to a rattle that was used during rituals for Hathor. Most of them typically had a U-shaped rattle with little cymbals strung from side to side. This sat on top of a handle some of which had a Hathor head on them. In this exercise you will make your very own sistrum with Hathor to guide you.

Supplies:
Tree branch in the shape of a "Y"
Bells, washers, buttons or bottle caps for sound
Floral wire
Wire-cutter
Sage bundle
One candle
Incense
Optional: paint, glitter, stick-on jewels, flowers

Before you start set up your altar with some sage, incense and and candle. Cleanse the area and your supplies with the sage and light your incense and candle. To invoke Hathor recite:

Hathor, Lady of Dance,

I call on you to aid me in creating a sacred sistrum
So that I may dance in your honor with your sacred instrument

Refer to the illustration above as a guide. Find a tree branch in the shape of a "Y" this will be the base for your sistrum. Thread your bells, bottles caps or buttons on the wire as this will be used to create the sound. Tie the wire with your rattling objects to each side of the "Y" so that it hangs in the middle. Now you can decorate your sistrum anyway you like either with paint, glitter, stick on jewels or whatever is appealing for you.

After you are finished creating your sacred rattle, cleanse it with the sage and recite:

Hathor, Mistress of Music
Bless this sistrum with your powers of music and dance
Let me dance in your honor while I play your sacred instrument
Mistress of Dance
I honor your ways

Thank Hathor for assisting you in this creation. Leave her an offering of perfume or perform a sacred dance in her honor with your sistrum. Keep your sistrum on your altar and use it when you perform your next ritual to Hathor.

Aphrodite, Greek Goddess of Love

Aphrodite was the Greek Goddess of love and passion and the most beautiful of the gods, although she represents much more than this. There is evidence of a goddess of love stemming back to the late Neolithic era. Most of the Neolithic figurines found were those of females with exaggerated breasts and stomach thought to represent fertility. There were also many bird goddesses as well as other animal goddesses. It is thought that many of these ancient representations were morphed into the more modern goddesses of Greek and Roman culture. Like the bird goddess, Aphrodite is also associated with doves and swans. The bird was seen as a sacred animal in Neolithic and ancient times. [1] Aphrodite was not a goddess associated with fertility, but with love and passion. She is the only goddess portrayed naked in ancient sculptures. She is often referred to as "The Golden One." [2]

Aphrodite is connected to deities such as the Sumerian Inanna who is associated with sexuality, as is Aphrodite. [3] Homer writes of Aphrodite as the smiling goddess, radiant and beautiful, much as how Sumerian poets described Inanna. [4] Aphrodite was also closely associated with the goddess Astarte, who is a sensuous goddess of sexuality. It is said that in her temples people would honor Astarte by making love, exactly like in the temples of Aphrodite later on. [5] It seems that over the centuries Aphrodite came to be as the goddesses before her, same attributes just with a different name and culture.

Daughter to Zeus, Father of the Gods, and Dione, a Mother Goddess, Aphrodite's creation myth says that she was born of sea foam impregnated by the heavens. She ended up floating ashore on the Greek islands where she was said to have been greeted by the Graces, her handmaidens. Aphrodite married Hephaestus, god of smith-craft, who was crippled. Aphrodite's passion is far too great to be with just one man, so she is known to have had many affairs. One of her most famous affairs was with

Adonis, god of beauty and desire. It is said that Aphrodite immediately fell in love with his beauty and youth. In order to keep him safe she decided to keep Adonis in a small trunk which she gave to Persephone, Queen of the Underworld. Persephone then ended up falling in love with Adonis and did not want to give him back to Aphrodite. The dispute between the two goddesses was settled by Zeus, Father of the Gods, and it was determined that Adonis would spend a third of the year by himself, a third of the year with Persephone and the rest with Aphrodite. Aphrodite would mourn the loss of her love each time he left. Adonis is said to have been killed by a wild boar and died in Aphrodite's arms. It is said that when he died, Aphrodite sprinkled a magical nectar in his blood so each year at spring the Adonis River, also known as the Abraham River, turns red in symbolic form of his magical blood. 6

Another of her famous lovers was Ares, god of war. Aphrodite and Ares had a long and intimate affair. She bore him four sons and one daughter. One night while they laid in lavish lovemaking on her husbands bed, the Sun God, Helios, saw them and sped off to Hephaestus to tell him of the affair. Hephaestus, hurt and ashamed, then began to angrily forge strong chains that could not be broken. He then went to the bedroom where Ares and Aphrodite lay, and bound them and the bed with the chains so all of the gods could see the lovers caught. Gods such as Poseidon, Hermes and Apollo, came to witness the shameful act, though no goddesses came to witness this because of the shame. There they stood laughing, and Hephaestus declared that Ares must pay. Poseidon disagreed and tried to talk Hephaestus into letting him go with the promise that he will pay for what he did. So he finally agreed and broke the chains to let the lovers go. Ares was sent to Thrace, and Aphrodite went to Cyprus. You can see in many of these myths the patriarchal view points coming through when it comes to goddesses of love.

Aphrodite's priestesses were said to be given to her temple to show their devotion to the goddess. Families would give their daughters and slave owners their slaves to honor the goddess of love. Her priestesses were sacred prostitutes, they were seen as the embodiment of Aphrodite, and by men making love with them this was seen as a sacred sexual union with the goddess. Sex and prostitution are viewed and practiced much differently today and these ideals were not present in the ancient world. 7

Aphrodite's festivals were usually in the spring and summer months. One of her many festivals, known as *Aphrodisia*, was celebrated around the Summer Solstice. This was known as a bathing festival where Aphrodite would go to her sacred bath at Paphos to be purified and adorned. It is also said that her daughter Peitho was honored and purified on this day as well. Although the *Aphrodisia* was said to be celebrated all through Greece, the main places for this ceremony was in Cyprus and Athens. 8 It is also said that at this celebration of purification and love, the temple would be purified and men would have intercourse with the Priestesses of Aphrodite, this was seen as a form of worship for the goddess. 9 It is said that the fourth day of every month was sacred to Aphrodite. 10 This would have been the fourth day after the new moon on the Athenian calendar. This day was essentially treated as an offering ceremony to give thanks and give back to the goddess for all she does. 11

The *Anagogia* was another of her festivals and was typically celebrated on the dark moon of May. The festival was said to take place on Mount Eryx, the site of one of Aphrodite's sacred temples. This seems to be a festival for navigation and embarking on the seas. The goddess is said to leave on a ship with her doves flying behind her, and she returns in nine days. There seems to be many festivals like this throughout the ancient world. 12

The festival of *Adonia* was held in honor of the death of Aphrodite's beloved Adonis. The goddess is said to have made this festival so the people would not forget his death or her mourning. Essentially, this was seen as a re-enactment of his funeral where women would make small wooden figures to be buried and they would cry at the loss of the beautiful god. The red rose is a sacred symbol at this festival to represent the blood that flowed from Adonis as he lay in the arms of Aphrodite, as well as the river of Adonis, which turns red each year to symbolize his sacred blood. 13

Aphrodite is the divine embodiment of love and passion. As is represented in her myths, passion can sometimes lead people astray, and the lust that comes along with it can get us into trouble. Love and passion know no boundaries, and the same would hold true for a goddess of love. Being that she is also the embodiment of beauty, and known as the most beautiful of the gods, she represents all the beauty in the natural world. Aphrodite is not the goddess to call upon when looking for a life partner since she rules passion. She is a great goddess to call upon for those seeking more love and passion in their current relationship, such as a marriage. In the following pages you will do exercises and a guided meditation to help you connect with this Goddess of Love.

Goddess Connections

Aphrodite teaches us about passionate love. She teaches us to love ourselves and to indulge in the beauties life has to offer. Aphrodite is the personification of raw sexual energy, she represents passionate lust and indulgence in one's sexuality. She can also invoke our passionate energy towards other areas of our life such as in our careers, ambitions and relationships. She lives life to its fullest treating herself to the all the beauty life has to offer. Aphrodite teaches us to stop and smell the flowers every so often as to not forget the beauty in our own lives. She can help the passion in a current relationship grow if it has been lost. Being the divine embodiment of beauty itself, she can also help us to see our own inner beauty.

Seeking Guidance in Aphrodite's Garden

Guided meditation is an essential part of connecting with your goddess. Not only does it relax your body, it also prepares your mind to connect to her energy. In this exercise you will take a journey to meet Aphrodite, and ask her for guidance for any issues that are troubling you.

Before any meditation make sure to ground and center yourself. Take some slow and deep breaths in and out a few times until you feel relaxed. You may also want to burn a smudge stick to cleanse the area. Once you feel centered you may start the meditation.

Imagine you are walking through a lush forest filled with trees and plants of all kinds. Beautiful green foliage surrounds you, the scent of sweet flowers is in the air. You hear doves cooing in the background and as you are walking you approach a huge and gorgeous temple. Tall pillars of glistening white with intricate designs stands before you. You enter the temple and are now in a sacred garden filled with roses of all kinds. Walk around and take it all in, breathe in the scent of the roses. There is a small marble bench off to the side and you walk over to sit down. Now invoke Aphrodite.

Recite:
Aphrodite lady of beauty
I invoke thee
In this beautiful garden of yours
I seek your guidance among the flowers

Something catches your attention by one of the rose bushes and when you glance over, Aphrodite is walking towards you with a red rose in her hand. She is magnificently beautiful and radiant, her knowing smile captures you. Once she is near you she takes the seat next to you. Embrace her and thank her for coming. She stands up and tells you to take a walk with her. You stand with her and the two of you walk around the garden together taking in the beauty around you. Now ask her whatever it is you need guidance for. Talk with her and pay attention to everything she says. Once she has answered your question, thank her again for coming. You embrace her once more and feel her passionate energy flowing through you. She gives you the rose she was holding and then she walks back through her sacred garden and disappears.

Now it is time for you to leave. Walk back through the garden and out the temple entrance. Continue walking down the forest path. Take a few deep breaths to come back. Once you feel ready, open your eyes and ground yourself. Take a few cleansing breaths and make sure to thank Aphrodite for her guidance. Leave a small offering of wine or a rose.

Write down your experience in your journal. Your answer may not come to you right away, but soon enough it will reveal itself to you. If you feel the need, practice this meditation a few times until you get a more concrete answer.

Discover your Inner Beauty Ritual with Aphrodite

Connecting with your inner beauty is an essential part of loving oneself. In a world filled with vanity and all types of beauty inducing products and even surgeries we forget that true beauty lies on the inside, not the outside. Learning to love oneself from the inside out is also a crucial part to learning how to love others. In order to love others we must first learn to love ourselves. In this ritual you will take a bath filled with beautiful and sweet smelling flowers and incense in order to invoke the beauty that lies within. Baths are also very therapeutic to body, mind and soul so this too shall help any inner healing.

Supplies:
Crushed rose petals
Candles

Sage bundle
Sweet smelling incense
Offering of honey or wine

Cleanse yourself and your area with your sage bundle. Pour crushed rose petals into the water, light your candle and incense and leave your offering. Once you're in the bath, ground and center yourself and recite:

Aphrodite, most beautiful Goddess of golden light
Lend me your confidence this waxing moon night,
Give me strength to discover my inner beauty
To honor and love myself truly
To be happy with who I really am
Teach me to cherish my body

Now immerse yourself in the warm water and meditate for a while. Imagine your body filling with a pink light from the inside out. Imaging yourself being filled with love. Hold this feeling for a few minutes. Once you're done meditating, when you feel it is sufficient, thank Aphrodite for her help and continue with your bath. Now you may finish your bath with whatever will continue to indulge you in beauty. You may choose to clean yourself with your favorite soap, exfoliate with a gentle scrub or even add some relaxing essential oils such as lavender to your bath to further relaxation. When you are finished with your bath make sure to put your favorite lotion or oil all over your body after you dry off. Everything you do in this ritual should be about continuing to feel beauty in whichever form that may be to you.

Be sure to record everything in your journal including any messages Aphrodite may have given you. This ritual can be performed once a week, or even everyday if you can, until you achieve your personal inner love goal.

Aphrodite's Creativity Charm

Aphrodite teaches us to indulge ourselves in life as often as we can. As a lover of beauty and indulgence herself, she understands that to enjoy and immerse yourself in beauty is essential at times in life. She surrounds herself with beautiful flowers and animals, sweet smelling perfumes, lovely food and wine, gorgeous jewelry as well as some of the other finer things in life. Aphrodite also teaches us to indulge ourselves in our passions and creativity to help us discover the beauty within. For this charm you will call upon Aphrodite to assist you in creating something of beauty, whatever that may be to you. Whether it be a piece of art, perfume, incense, jewelry or even a special meal, whatever will invoke your creativity.

Once you have decided on what to make, gather your supplies and set everything up so you are ready to make it. This ritual should be performed on the full moon so your creativity will be at its fullest

Supplies:
Candle
Sage bundle
Rose or vanilla incense
Offering of red rose

Cleanse your space with sage, light your candle and incense, center and ground yourself. Recite:

Aphrodite, beautiful and passionate muse
I call on your passionate powers this full moon
Inspire my creative abilities within
Help me to create this (what you are creating)
Show me your beauty through what I create

Beautiful one, so lovely and great!

Now start to make your special item. Feel free to play calming music in the background, light candles or anything that might add to the beauty of your surroundings. After you have finished with your creation bless it in the name of Aphrodite so that when you wear it, eat it, display it etc., you are reminded of the beauty in your creativity.

Hekate, Greek Goddess of the Crossroads

Hekate is a Greek goddess associated with magic, witchcraft, necromancy, childbirth and crossroads. She is a liminal goddess, one who dwells in the in-between places. Hekate is ruler of the three realms Earth, Sea and Sky. 1 Daughter to Perses and Asteria, Hekate is said to have originated in Anatolia and some of the earliest signs of her worship are also found in Caria and Thrace. Her sacred temple in Lagina is located in South Western Turkey, so it seems her worship was spread throughout the ancient world. She was also worshiped in Rome. 2

Some of her myths say that she was pre-olympian. Others say that she was the daughter of Zeus. Hekate is seen as a dark goddess, sometimes known as a crone. Although, she is actually a triple goddess, her crone aspect has shown through the most, due to negative views placed on her. Mostly because of her great wisdom and her no nonsense attitude, which was feared by the new religion. So they turned her into a crone hoping to take some of her appeal away. Although still today many people pray to Hekate. She is seen as the Great Illuminator, lighting our path with her flaming torches. She helps us to let go of that which no longer serves us, so we can take our true path. She is a strong and powerful goddess. 3

Hekate fills many roles as a goddess. Some of her popular titles are:

Phosphorus: Light-bearer
Soteira: Saviour
Kleidouchos: Key bearer
Triformis: Three bodied
Enodia: Of the ways

She was often depicted in triple form holding a snake, a dagger and her famous torches. Sometimes one of her heads is that of a dog or snake. 4 She represents the darker side of life and of ourselves. To truly be whole and accepting of ourselves, we must know our entire self, including our darker aspects. Hekate helps us to identify what we need to let go of, and shed our old skin so to speak. Although she can not do it for us, it is our choice to make.

As a goddess of many realms, Hekate has access to the Underworld as well. She appears in the myth of Demeter and Persephone. Every year she guides Persephone back down to the Underworld where Persephone spends half the year with her husband Hades. In this myth you can see her role as "light-bearer" in that even in the most darkest of times, Hekate's light will shine. Hekate also identified with many other goddesses such as Selene, goddess of the moon, and Artemis, goddess of the hunt. Some say these goddesses were looked at as a triad of goddesses. Hecate - Artemis - Selene. In myth of the witch Medea, who was a devotee to Hekate, was said to pray to these goddesses as triple formed. 5

Hekate's cults were widespread. There is said to be evidence of her worship in a cave on the island of Samothrace, which is a Greek island located in the Aegean Sea. Evidence of her worship was also found in Attika and Eleusis which was a town in Attika. Hekate was one of the goddesses involved in the Eleusinian mysteries, which deals with the story of Persephone's abduction to the Underworld. Also in Thrace which is North of Greece, it is said the Hekate was closely associated with the Thracian goddess, Bendis. In Aigina, which is an island not too far off the coast from Athens, it is said "*Of the gods, the Aiginetans worship most Hekate, in whose honor every year they celebrate mystic rites*". This quote comes from the writings of the Greek geographer *Pausanias* in his *Description of Greece 2. 30. 2* which was around the second century CE. She was worshiped in many other places as well; her devotees were very widespread. 6

Like many cultures in the ancient world, the Greeks were known for their lavish rituals and festivals in honor of their gods. Hekate had monthly rituals which were held in her honor on the dark moon and the new moon. On the dark moon a ritual known as *Deipnon* was held in honor of Hekate where people would partake in *Hekate Suppers*. 7 These were basically elaborate food offerings left to Hekate at a crossroads on the last night of the lunar month which was the dark moon in the Greek calendar.

Before the food offerings were prepared, people would clean their houses from top to bottom along with the household shrines. They would also cleanse themselves in order to be pure for the return of the new moon the following days.

They would then take their food out to a crossroads and eat their dinner under the dark moon, and leave a plate for the goddess. These meals usually consisted of eggs, fish, mushrooms, garlic and honey cakes. They might also leave flaming torches, or put candles in the honey cakes. This was also a night where restless spirits were said to roam the earth seeking vengeance. Because of this Hekate is also associated with the dead and the Underworld. This combined with the food offerings left at a crossroads is thought to link Hekate with primitive death cult practices. 8

The *Noumenia* was held the following day on the new moon at the beginning of the month. Hekate was honored on this day because it is said that she gives good omens on this day. This is a good day to practice magic or divination. 9 Another festival that is thought to have been associated with Hekate was the *Nemoralia* also known as the Festival of Torches. This was a Roman celebration held on the full moon around the month of August and was traditionally a festival for the goddess Diana. Although in modern times people honor Hekate on this day because of the relation of the two goddesses and the symbolism in the festival. Worshipers would carry torches and form a procession of lights around lake Nemi and it is said that dogs were also honored on this day. 10

Hekate has a different message and purpose for each of us. She may also appear differently to some, and you may connect with certain aspects of her that others don't. She will show you the part of her that you most need. In the following pages you will do exercises and a guided meditation to help you connect with this Goddess of the Crossroads.

Goddess Connections

Hekate is a goddess that will show us the darker aspects of ourselves. She helps us to let go of that which no longer serves us, such as negative baggage that we have accumulated throughout our lives. Sometimes, coming to terms with the more negative and darker aspects of ourselves can be a very difficult and trying experience. She serves as our light-bearer in helping us to not only identify our darker aspects, but also in understanding them and overcoming them. You have to be ready to shed your old skin, so you can start on your new path with confidence. She will help you come to terms with and accept the person you truly are. She is also a goddess of crossroads, holds the key to wisdom, and can help guide you down your chosen path. She will not give you the exact answer you seek, that is up to you to find out. She will however steer you in the right direction and teach you how to use your own intuition to make the choices that are right for you.

Guided Meditation to Meet Hekate

Guided meditation is an essential part of connecting with your goddess. Not only does it relax your body, it also prepares your mind to connect with her energy. In this exercise, you will take a journey to meet Hekate, and ask her for guidance for any issues that are troubling you.

Before any meditation make sure to ground and center yourself. Take some slow and deep breaths in and out a few times until you feel relaxed. You may also want to burn a smudge stick to cleanse the area. Once you feel centered you may start the meditation.

Imagine that you are in a lush forest surrounded by trees. You hear birds chirping and there is a light breeze on your face. You start to walk down a path, hearing the leaves crunching under your feet, until you come to a wooden door. You open the door, and go inside. Once you're through the door, you find yourself in a long hallway with many doors. It is somewhat dark and you can't see very well. At this point you invoke Hekate.

Recite:
Hekate, bearer of torches,
I invoke your power of light in this moment of darkness.

At the end of the hall you faintly see two lights coming towards you. As the lights get closer, you start to see the Great Goddess Hekate manifesting before your very eyes. (let whatever image you create of her come through naturally don't force an image of her). As she is now standing before you, holding her flaming torches, thank her for coming to help you with your issue at hand. Tell her what you brought her here for, and what is troubling you about your situation. (Take a few minutes to explain this to her, and listen to see if she has anything to say)

Hekate then asks you to hold out your hand and close your eyes. She puts something in your hand, and says, *"This will give you the answer you seek".* When you open your eyes, she is gone and in your hand lies a key. As you look up again noticing all the doors in the long hallway, you realize that your answer is behind one of those doors. (Take a moment to decide which door to choose). Now choose your door and open it with your key.

Go inside the room and pay close attention to whatever is going on in there. (Take a few moments to really take it all in and remember everything you saw) Now come back out into the hallway, and go back through the original wooden door you came through. Go back out into the forest and walk back down the path. Take a few deep breaths to come back. Once you feel ready, open your eyes and ground yourself. Take a few cleansing breaths and make sure to thank Hekate for her guidance. Leave a small offering of honey.

Write down your experience in your journal. Your answer may not come to you right away, but soon enough it will reveal itself to you. If you feel the need, practice this meditation a few times until you get a more concrete answer.

Letting Go Ritual with Hekate

In this exercise you will do a ritual to banish something negative from your life. Since Hekate is the goddess of letting go, you will invoke her power to help you let go of something negative that no longer serves you. This can be anything including people, jobs, habits, ways of thinking or anything you want to let go of. Anything that no longer serves you in a positive way.

Supplies:
A small piece of paper
One candle
Sage bundle
Cauldron/fire proof bowl
Incense
Offering

Cleanse yourself and your area with sage. Light your candle and incense. Now visualize what it is you want to banish. Take your piece of paper and write on it what you want to banish. Start with just one thing. Banishing more than one thing at a time can lead to less focus. Now recite the following prayer.

Recite:
Hekate, I invoke your presence
Help me to release this negativity
So that I may be cleansed and free

Hold your piece of paper over the flame of the candle and recite:
(Say what you want to banish)

I release you from my life and from my mind.

Burn the paper and throw it in the fireproof dish. Imagine your negativity burning and turning to ashes. Visualize your bad habit burning away with the smoke. Meditate for a few moments. Thank Hekate and leave your offering. Let the candle burn down completely and bury the ashes in the earth. Make sure to record everything in your journal.

Deipnon Ritual for Hekate

Deipnon was the last day of the Greek lunar calendar, and it was also the dark moon. On this day people would clean their houses and keep their dust or dirt to leave at a crossroads. It was also a night to leave food offerings for Hekate at a crossroads. These were known as Hekate Suppers. This was basically a whole day of cleansing, and praying to Hekate for blessings for the next month. At night people would leave their food offerings and their home cleanings at a crossroads for the goddess. They made sure to separate the food offerings from the home cleanings.

In this exercise you will be performing a Deipnon ritual which is to be held on the dark moon. Take the day (or as much as you can) for cleaning your home. Make sure it's a good and thorough cleaning. Floors, counters, anywhere you see dust, or any areas you might not clean as often. Organize things, maybe that closet you've been thinking of cleaning. Any home altars or shrines were cleaned on this day as well. So clean your shrines, refresh your offerings, clean off your statues, and make your altars are nice and clean. Keep your dirt, dust, etc. to leave outside or at a crossroads if you so wish.

After you've cleaned your house, you should also cleanse yourself with a nice bath or shower. Now you may set up an altar to Hekate.

Supplies:
White candle

Sage bundle

Incense

Food offerings: cheesecake, eggs, garlic, small cakes, honey (you can choose as many or as little of these as you wish)

Make sure you put the food offerings on your altar as well to bless them. Cleanse yourself and your area with sage. Light your candle and incense. Take a few deep, slow breaths in an out to center yourself. Now recite:

Hekate, Ancient Goddess of night,
I honor you on this Deipnon,
Bless this house with your shining light,
And keep us safe until the next moon.

Now stand up with your smudge stick and walk around your house spreading the sage smoke around while chanting what you recited to Hekate. When you're done, you may place your smudge stick back on your altar, make sure to spread some over your food offerings well. Thank Hekate for her blessings.

Take your food offerings and the dust/dirt from your house cleaning outside. You can simply take these to your backyard or if you have access to a crossroads somewhere safe you can take it there too. Make sure when you leave your offerings, you take your food out of any wrappings or anything that's not natural. You are leaving this food on the earth and animals will come and eat it, so you want to keep that in mind. Make sure what you're leaving is safe for the earth and all of her creatures. Also keep in mind that if you do leave your offerings in your backyard this will attract ants and other bugs or even rodents so be sure to clean it up as soon as you can.

After you've left your offerings for Hekate, thank her again and return home. Make sure to have a nice dinner yourself, for tomorrow is a new day, and the new moon. This is known as Noumenia and people would pray to Hekate on this day as well. Check your offerings the next day and clean up anything that was left behind. Make sure to record everything in your journal. You may want to perform the Deipnon every month to become closer to Hekate.

Artemis, Greek Goddess of the Hunt

Artemis is known as a virgin goddess of the hunt, the forest and animals, the new moon and femininity. Greek in origin, her parents are said to be the goddess Leto and the god Zeus. Artemis also had a twin brother Apollo, god of the sun and the two were often worshiped together. It is thought that Artemis may have originated from a Minoan goddess, *Potnia Theron* or *Lady of the Beasts* as the two share similar qualities. 1 Artemis is also a goddess of childbirth and is said to have helped her mother give birth to her brother Apollo shortly after she herself was born. 2

Artemis was often depicted as being tall and beautiful and carrying her bow and arrows. Many ancient statues made in her likeness depict her with her quiver of arrows and bow running with her dog companions or a stag at her side. Quite befitting of a huntress. 3 She is said to have been deeply desired by many of the gods and was courted by many of them as well. 4 Although she is known as a virgin goddess, she is known to have had a companion and possible lover. Orion, a mortal hunter is said to have captured the heart of Artemis. The two met while hunting and quickly became companions. Although Artemis's brother Apollo did not approve of their relationship. He sent a scorpion to fight Orion and then tricked Artemis into killing him. She then placed his body among the stars as a tribute to their friendship. 5

In myth it is said that Leto became pregnant with her twins by Zeus, father of the gods. Although Zeus had been married to Hera at the time and when Hera found out that Leto was pregnant she became filled with furious rage. She sent the Python of Delphi after Leto who chased her off the land preventing her from stopping to rest or give birth anywhere. Hera also forced different rulers of the land to not give Leto sanctuary. Finally Zeus came to her rescue and helped Leto seek refuge on the island of Delos and this is where she gave birth to her twins, Artemis and Apollo 6

Artemis appears in many of the Ancient Greek myths such as the story of the sacrifice of Iphigeneia. This story is about a young mortal girl who became a priestess of Artemis and some versions also say that she was made immortal as well. Iphigeneia was the daughter of King Agememnon who was the leader of the Greek forces in the Trojan war. King Agememmon is said to have offended Artemis after he declared himself the greatest of hunters after killing a deer. Artemis is said to have prevented his ships from sailing by stilling the wind. She said that she would not let him sail again until he sacrificed his most beautiful daughter Iphigeneia. Agememnon took his daughter to be sacrificed and placed her on the altar. At the last moment Artemis turned her into a deer and took her to safe refuge at her temple. She is said to have made the girl one of her priestesses. 7

Another myth is that of the story of Callisto who was a princess of Lycaon in Arcadia. It is said that Callisto swore herself to Artemis stating that she would be a virgin forever and a loyal servant to her goddess. Although one day Zeus saw Callisto and he became filled with desire for her. He forced himself on the princess making her pregnant. Callisto tried to hide her pregnant belly from Artemis but one day the goddess saw Callisto bathing and discovered that she was pregnant. Artemis became enraged and turned Callisto into a bear. She then proceeded to hunt and kill her. Zeus is said to have taken the unborn child and gave it to the goddess Maia. He named the child *Arkas* or bear. During his mourning for Callisto he decided to place her in the stars and she became the constellation *Arktos* or bear which is now known as *Ursa Major* or *Big Bear*. 8

Artemis was associated with goddesses from other pantheons as well. She was closely associated with the Egyptian goddess Isis and in some parts of Egypt the goddess Isis was known as *Isis-Artemis*. She was also associated with the Roman goddess Diana and the Greek goddess Hekate. 9
There were many sanctuaries and temples for this virgin huntress. The most famous being her temple in Ephesus which later became one of the Seven Wonders of the Ancient World. Her temples were said to stretch as far as Anatolia, Sicily and Gaul. Artemis had many festivals celebrated at these temples in her honor. The Greeks were known for their lavish

festivals in honor of their beloved gods. The Greek calendar was different from our modern day calendar as they were revolved around the sun and phases of the moon. It's hard to pinpoint the exact dates of the festivals but we do know the ancient names of the months in which they were celebrated.

The festival *Elaphebolia* was celebrated during the month *Elaphebolion*. Cakes made of dough, honey and sesame seeds were made in the shape of a stag and given to Artemis as an offering. 10 The festival *Thargelia* was celebrated on the 6th and 7th day of the month *Thargelion* in honor of the birth of Artemis and Apollo. 11 Another festival held in honor of Artemis was the *Mounykhia* which was celebrated during the month of *Mounykhion*. This celebration was held in honor of Artemis-Hekate and was held during the full moon. Small cakes were made with tiny candles or "little torches" and offered to the goddess. These same cakes were also given to Hekate during her festivals. 12 These are just some of the festivals held in her honor.

Artemis was a beloved goddess to the Greeks which is reflected in the many myths she is involved in and her widespread temple locations. In the following pages you will do exercises and a guided meditation to help you connect with this Goddess of Nature.

Goddess Connections

Artemis teaches us how to be strong and independent. She shows us that in order to fully connect with ourselves we must sometimes seek solitude in nature. That we must accept our flaws and mistakes as lessons which teach us to be strong. Artemis guides us to knowing ourselves better and to thriving on our own. She is a symbol of freedom and she shows us how to live our lives more freely. She teaches us to connect with nature and watch it closely in order to receive insight. She tells us that in order to hear your inner voice you must first seek out quite solitude. Artemis shows us how to be strong when we face adversity. For it is in our experiences of bad and good that we grow and learn and experience our lessons of wisdom.

Guided Meditation to Meet Artemis

Guided meditation is an essential part of connecting with your goddess. Not only does it relax your body, it also prepares your mind to connect with her energy. In this exercise you will take a journey to meet Artemis and ask her for guidance for any issues that are troubling you.

Before any meditation make sure to ground and center yourself. Take some slow and deep breaths in and out a few times until you feel relaxed. You may also want to burn a smudge stick to cleanse the area. Once you feel centered you may start the meditation.

Imagine that you are in a dense forest with tall bushy trees. You are walking along a path and taking in all the beauty around you. The sun is shining above you and the rays are coming through the trees illuminating your path. You stop to feel the wind blowing which rustles the leaves on the trees. Listen to the birds sing and observe any animals that may be around you. Off in the distance you hear a branch crack on the forest floor. You glance over and see a magnificent stag with broad antlers standing before you. You dare not to move lest you may scare it off. The deer looks into your eyes and beckons you to follow him. He then starts walking away slowly and you follow.

The stag starts to pick up speed trotting through the forest and now he's bounding around the trees with his nimble legs. Finally, he stops in a clearing and you notice that there is a lake there. The stag bends down to drink some water and you join him. When you get back up you notice that there is a beautiful woman standing on the other side of the lake. She has her hair pulled back, a crescent moon on her brow and she's carrying a bow and arrow. She calls the stag over to her and the stag wades through the shallow lake over to her. She then calls to you as well and you follow in the stag's footsteps. Once you reach her you realize that this beautiful woman of the forest is the goddess Artemis. You stare at her in awe and take in her wild looking nature. You then look to the stag and thank it for bringing you to the goddess and the stag leaps off into the forest. You embrace Artemis and tell her how honored you are to be in her presence.

She tells you to walk with her through the trees. At this point the sun has set and you look up into the star filled night sky and see a tiny crescent moon over head. Artemis tells you that it's time to honor the wild woman within yourself. That it's time to claim your independence and freedom. She then takes off running through the forest and you start after her. You're running in between trees feeling the leaves brush against your face. All of a sudden a pack of dogs is running at your side. You all run and leap through the forest as though you were nimble deer yourselves.

All of a sudden Artemis stops as do her dogs. She crouches down into the brush and you do the same. She points to a lone stag off in the distance. She teaches you to be still and observe the beauty of the forest and all the animals within it. She shows you the freedom that comes with being a wild woman and a huntress. The stag notices you staring at it and it leaps off back into the forest. Artemis stands up tall and tells you that in order to reclaim your wild woman self and your freedom you must spend time in nature. She says that you must observe the animals in nature and be one with them. You must run with the deer and hunt with the dogs. You must be still and quiet in order to listen to your inner wild woman. She takes her bow from her back and a single arrow out of its case and hands it to you. "These are your wild woman tools. Your symbols of freedom and independence. Use them wisely."

You then thank Artemis for imparting all of this wisdom upon you. She embraces you once more before she and her dogs take off again and disappear into the forest. You start to walk back through the forest back to the lake. Now slowly take a few deep breaths to come back. Once you feel ready, open your eyes and ground yourself. Take a few cleansing breaths, and make sure to thank Artemis for her guidance.

Write down your experience in your journal. Your answer may not come to you right away, but soon enough it will reveal itself to you. If you feel the need, practice this meditation a few times until you get a more concrete answer.

Nature Connection Ritual with Artemis

Artemis represents the wildness in nature, independence and feelings of freedom. She runs through the forest with a deer at her side as if she was one with her beloved animals. She is also the huntress and carries her bow and arrows for her protection. Since Artemis is incredibly associated with nature it is imperative to be in nature at some point in order to fully connect with her wild energy. In this exercise you will do just that.

Find a place where you can be in nature. It can be the beach, the mountains, a forest, a local park or your own backyard if you don't have access to a nature setting. For this exercise it's better to be alone in order to better connect with your independence. I find that the most potent times for magic in nature or the best times to see animals are at dawn and dusk. Before you go, cleanse yourself with some sage and clear your mind for a few minutes with a short meditation concentrating on your breath. This will cleanse your body, mind and soul and prepare you for your adventure. Once you're ready take your journey to your nature spot.

Once you've arrived take a good look around and try to find a peaceful area if possible. First walk around and take in all the sights and sounds. Take notice of any animals in the area. Feel the wind on your face. Breathe in any smells and listen to any natural sounds like birds singing or leaves rustling in the wind. Fully immerse yourself in your surroundings. Take it all in. You may wish to walk the whole time or you may wish to find a peaceful place to sit. Once you feel the energy of the natural setting around you, recite the following prayer.

Artemis, wild woman and nature lover
Allow me to be filled with your wildness
Allow me to be filled with your independence
Allow me to feel the freedom that comes with being independent

Fill up my soul with your strength
I wish to run free at your side
This I ask of you
As I will it, so shall it be

On your way out of your nature setting look around for anything that may speak to you. It could be anything natural like a leaf, a shell, a feather or a rock. This is a message from Artemis and if you do decide to take back your nature token be sure to thank our Mother Earth for her generous offering to you. Once you arrive back home, place your nature token on your altar and write about your experience in your journal. Pay attention to your dreams that night as the goddess may send messages to you in your sleep. Anytime you need to reconnect with the energy of Artemis you may repeat this exercise. Although I would not recommend taking a nature token every time. You may also wish to bring an offering for Artemis to leave at your sacred nature area, just make sure that it is also natural.

Find your Power Animal with Artemis

Artemis is deeply connected to the animals and the land. She is in a sense a nature goddess, a version of the Lady of Beasts. She can in turn help us to better connect with and understand animals. In this ritual you will ask Artemis to help you in connecting with your power or spirit animal. Connecting with your power animal will help you to better understand yourself and your goddess. Once you discover your power animal you may call on their energy in rituals just like you would a deity. This ritual is best performed at night before bed as part of it involves dreaming.

Supplies:
Candle
Incense

Sage bundle
Offering of honey or wildflowers

Set up your altar with your candle, incense and your offering. Light your sage bundle and cleanse yourself and your area with the smoke. Take a few deep breaths in and out and center yourself. Once you feel ready, recite:

Artemis Lady of the wild land
She who runs with dogs and stags
Wild Woman of nature
Help me to discover my power animal
The animal who will guide me
The wild animal of my spirit
This I ask of you
As I will it
So shall it be

Meditate for a few minutes to see if any images come to your mind. Go with the first animal image you see, don't be disappointed if it's not an animal you necessarily want. Your power animal can change over the course of your life and you may even have more than one at one point. I believe that the animal you need most at a point in your life is the one who will show itself to you. If you get any images remember them and thank Artemis for her guidance. Slowly come out of the meditation with a few slow and deep breaths. Once you feel ready open your eyes and record everything in your journal. Now if you didn't receive any images during your meditation you still may receive some in your dreams. Keep your journal next to your bed and take note of your dreams. Once you discover your power animal you may want to do a little research to find out what their energy means for your life.

Freyja, Norse Goddess of Beauty and War

Freyja is the Norse Goddess of beauty, war and fertility. She was a very prominent and powerful Goddess in the Norse culture. She is one of the *Vanir*, which are a race of gods and goddesses who live in Vanaheim. It is said that they were the original gods. The leaders of the *Vanir* were Freyja and her brother Freyr. They were fertility gods who gave peace and abundance. They also brought their knowledge of magic and witchcraft. There is another race of Norse gods known as the *Aesir* who were at war with the *Vanir* for a while. This was known as the first war in the world. Being that both races, the *Vanir* and the *Aesir*, were both strong and talented in many areas of warfare and magic, they fought for a very long time and it looked like neither side would win. They decided to call a truce and live peacefully side by side. They even agreed to exchange some of their leaders as proof of their dedication. 1

Daughter to Njord, Freyja was often depicted with long blonde hair, blue eyes and wearing the famous *Brigasgamen* necklace around her neck. This beloved necklace of hers was made of amber and rubies and was crafted by four dwarves. When Freyja saw the necklace she immediately fell in love and had to have it. The dwarves agreed to give her this magnificent necklace, on one condition. That she spend a night with each of them. So Freyja did as she was instructed and got her prized possession. 2

She was said to own a magical cloak made from falcon feathers which enabled her to soar the skies and look down upon the land. On one occasion she used this magical cloak to search for her beloved husband. Freyja was married to the god Od, the sun god. It is said in a myth that one day her husband disappeared and Freyja was distraught. She wept as she soared across the sky searching for him. As her tears fell to the land they turned to amber and when they fell in the sea they turned to gold. 3 Both of these are sacred to her.

She was also known to have a battle boar that she rode named Hildisvini. In one tale, Freyja rode her boar to the cave were the Giantess Hyndla slept to try and convince her to come with Freyja to Valhalla where Odin was. When Hyndla laid eyes on Fryeja's boar she said *"That's no boar, that's your lover Ottar! You're riding your lover on the road to Valhalla!"* Freyja denied it at the time, although later confessed to the Giantess that it was Ottar, her lover. 4 As well as a boar, Freyja also had a chariot led by cats which is another sacred animal of Freyja.

Freyja was also known as being a practitioner of magic. She was considered a goddess of magic and sometimes referred to as a witch. The Norse had an ancient magical practice much like shamanism that was called *Seidr*. Freyja was a practitioner of this magic. *Seidr* involved rituals with trance-like states where the practitioners would be taken on a journey to the other-world. It also involved what would be known as spell work today, divination, and herb lore. 5 Sometimes in a *Seidr* ritual the priestess, known as the *Volva*, would be put into a trance-like state, and then act as a prophetic messenger and seeress to the rest of the group. People would ask questions and she would give them answers from her trance prophecies. 6 Very much like the Oracle of Delphi and any other known prophetesses. Some myths say Freyja even taught the art of *Seidr* to the god Odin, even though it was a mostly female practice.

In the Norse culture, upon the death of warriors in battle, the slain were divided up between two halls. Odin's at Valhalla, and Freyja's at Folkvang. The dead were taken by the Valkyries who were dark angels that would soar over battlefields to gather up the fallen heroes to bring back to Valhalla, the heavenly realm of Odin. The Valkyries, known as the *"choosers of the slain",* were seen as beautiful women with long flowing hair who would serve mead to the chosen dead heroes in the hall of Valhalla. Since Freyja had her own death hall, it would be appropriate to say that Freyja was also a goddess of battle and death. Some myths say that Freyja was the leader of the Valkyries, but some scholars dispute this fact saying that there isn't enough evidence to support this theory. 7

Some stories talk about Freyja being a promiscuous goddess, although it is not known for sure since many of the people who wrote the Norse myths were Christian. Most of the information we have about the Norse cultures comes from the Poetic and Prose Edda's, which are collections of stories and poems about the Norse culture. Snorri Sturluson, who is the author of the Prose Edda, was a Christian living in the 1200's. 8 It's hard to decipher the actual myths of the Viking gods and goddesses through the writing of a Christian, because there is no way to tell what was added or changed to make the Norse deities look bad. For that reason, study of real ancient Norse mythology has been a somewhat difficult process for scholars and authors alike.

There were no actual dates for the Norse festivals per se. Rather they had seasonal festivals a few times throughout the year. These festivals were called *blots* and many different gods and goddesses were honored at each one. It is known to be traditional to honor Freyja at Yule, and also during the Spring. These feasts held in honor of the season's and the god's, consisted of animal sacrifices in which they would cook and eat the meat that was sacrificed. The blood from these animals was thought to contain magical powers. Because of this it was sprinkled on the statues of the god's, and on the participants themselves. Today this whole act would be seen as gruesome and totally unacceptable. Although it is a part of our history, and the history of the Norse people so I find it relevant to mention here.

Mead was a very important part of any blot. Goblets filled with mead had to be drunk in honor of each god or goddess being celebrated. They also were known to have big bonfires and feast all night long. 9 Although it is not appropriate in our world today to sacrifice any living thing for any ritual, it was a very common practice in the ancient world, and all over the ancient world.

To really understand Freyja, studying the rest of the Norse gods is almost essential. You can learn much about Freyja, but the Norse gods are so intertwined with each other it's hard to learn about one without learning at least a little about the others. So sometimes when you're honoring Freyja, leave a small offering for Odin, Thor, or Frigg as well. The Norse gods like offering's and a little appreciation can go along way with this pantheon of gods. In the following pages you will do exercises and a guided meditation to help you connect with this Goddess of Beauty.

Goddess Connections

Freyja teaches us to be strong, independent and courageous. We can lead the battles of our own lives and lead them with confidence. She also teaches us to be playful at times, and indulge in the pleasures life has to offer. Being a goddess of beauty, who was also beautiful, she also shows us how to appreciate the beauty in life and in ourselves. To fully life live and treat yourselves to the abundant beauty all around you. She is invoked in matters of fertility, love and passion. She helps us to have more passion in our lives and towards the things and people we love.

Guided Meditation to meet Freyja

Guided meditation is an essential part of connecting with your goddess. Not only does it relax your body, it also prepares your mind to connect to her energy. In this exercise you will take a journey to meet Freyja, and ask her for guidance for any issues that are troubling you.

Before any meditation make sure to ground and center yourself. Take some slow and deep breaths in and out a few times until you feel relaxed. You may also want to burn a smudge stick to cleanse the area. Once you feel centered you may start the meditation.

Imagine that you are in a meadow with green rolling hills covered in wildflowers. The sun is shining down on your face and you feel the breeze through your hair. As you are walking along enjoying the scenery you notice a grassy mound with a wooden door covered in beautiful ornate carvings. You open the door and step inside. Now you notice that you are in a different place. Where snow is covering the landscape and you hear people and children off in the distance. They are laughing and playing music and it seems a celebration of sorts is being held.

A beautiful gray cat appears and approaches you. When you bend down to pet it, she takes off running. Though she doesn't go too far. She stops and looks back at you so you follow her. She continues on going through the forest, pouncing with ease through the snow. She stops every so often to look back at you. Almost as if she's making sure you are still following her. She takes you through a small stream stepping on rocks to get across when finally, she stops. You bend down to pet her and you notice her collar. There is a rune on her collar, the rune Fehu, Freyja's rune. You start to rub the rune, and you close your eyes feeling it's energy. You start to chant (say aloud 3 times) *Freyja, Goddess of love and war, I invoke your presence, be with me now.*

When you open your eyes, you notice a falcon has landed on a tree next to you. As you stand up the falcon starts to transform. All of a sudden, standing there is a beautiful woman with long blond hair, a necklace made of amber and rubies, and she is wearing a magical cloak of falcon feathers. You realize, she is Freyja. Overcome with joy that she has shown herself to you, you greet her. She extends out her hand to you, you take it and she pulls you close to her. She then wraps her magical falcon cloak around you both, and the two of you take off towards the sky.

Now both of you have transformed into falcons. Soaring side by side as falcons, you notice the world below you. You can see everything so clearly from up here. You may take this time to speak with Freyja about a problem you're having, or you can choose to soar with her feeling her energy and let your vision unfold. After a little while, you both soar back down to earth and are transformed back to yourself. You look up at Freyja, and she says *"Remember what I've taught you"*. She then turns back into a falcon, and flies away.

As you turn around to head back, you notice the gray cat is there to lead you the way back over the stream and through the snow where she stops in front of the magical door you entered through. You bend down to pet her and thank her for her help and guidance. Walk back through the door. Take a few deep breaths to come back. Once you feel ready, open your eyes and ground yourself. Take a few cleansing breaths and make sure to thank Freyja for her guidance. Leave a small offering of honey or amber.

Write down your experience in your journal. Your answer may not come to you right away, but soon enough it will reveal itself to you. If you feel the need, practice this meditation a few times until you get a more concrete answer.

Invoke your passions with Freyja

This ritual's purpose is to increase your passion, drive or ambition in a certain area of your life that's lacking these qualities. As you already know, Freyja is an ambitious and passionate Goddess, and she can teach us to be the same with our personal endeavors in life. Whether it be more passion you need towards a creative project, a relationship, a business venture, or any other area of your life that is lacking passion or ambition.

Supplies:
Candle
Incense
Sage bundle
Offering of wine or honey

To begin cleanse your area and yourself with your sage bundle. Visualize what area of your life you need more passion or ambition in. Take a few slow and deep breaths in and out to center yourself. Light your candle and incense, and invoke Freyja. Recite:

Freyja, Beautiful Goddess of the Vanir,
I invoke your powers of passion and ambition
I ask that you lend me these powers in (insert what area of your life and what
exactly it is you want it for).
So that I may accomplish my goals
And live the life I was destined to live
As I will it
So shall it be

Now visualize yourself living your passion and accomplishing your goal. Hold this vision for a few minutes and really feel what it would be like to accomplish your goal. Stay in this moment and immerse yourself in that feeling. Imagine yourself accomplishing your goal and imagine yourself after you've accomplished it. Meditate for a little while and then ask Freyja if she has any messages for you. She may or may not have anything for you. Once you feel ready, slowly come out of your meditation and thank Freyja for her guidance. Leave her an offering of wine or honey. Make sure to record everything in your journal.

Sacred Norse Blot with Freyja

In the Norse culture their festivals were called blots. They were usually seasonal festivals that sometimes included the whole village, and sometimes they would be more personal. Each blot had different gods and goddesses associated with them. What usually took place at a blot was a sacrifice, then an invocation to the particular gods, and then a big sacramental feast was held in celebration of the particular season. Unfortunately, animal sacrifice was a part of our ancient world, and in many cultures from the Norse to the Romans to the Greeks and so on. So of course when practicing a modern form of a blot there would be no animal sacrifice!

Typical food and drink consumed at these seasonal feasts consisted of mead, meat, fish, eggs and breads. Mead was a very important and sacred part of all the blots. But you can choose your own menu as far as food goes. Meat was a very traditional part of the festivals but of course some of us don't eat meat. So choose your menu based on your normal eating habits while adding as much or as little traditional fare as you feel comfortable.

After the blot feast was over, the people of the household would make a small plate of food to put outside for the household "*nisse*" or fairy. They believed the *nisse* was the protector and guardian of the household and would show their appreciation by leaving a small offering for them. 9 In this modern day blot to Freyja, you are going to set up your altar, recite a prayer and give your offering, which will be a sacrificial cake of some kind. Then you would have a feast (or small dinner) and then set out a small plate of food for the *nisse*. You can choose to do this ceremony either on one of the seasonal festival days, or on the waxing of full moon.

For your feast you can decide to invite over friends and have a big celebration, or if you want something small and intimate then just have a family dinner as you normally would.

Supplies:
One candle
Incense
Sage bundle
Small sacrificial cake (either home-made or store bought, it can even be a cupcake or muffin)
Mead
Feast or dinner afterwards.

Set up your altar with your candle, incense, sacrificial cake and the mead. Cleanse yourself and your area with the sage. Light your candle and incense.

Recite:

Freyja, Goddess of Beauty and War,
I light this candle, and have this sacred feast in your honor.
On this night of (insert moon phase or seasonal day) I say this prayer,
And drink to you.
Lady of beauty and magic, take this cake (hold cake over candle flame) as an
offering (place cake back on altar).
On this sacred day,
Freyja, woman of amber and gold,
I honor you on this festival of old!

Now it's time to have your feast/dinner! While eating your dinner make a toast to Freyja to honor her. After your feast, take your sacrificial cake and a small portion of your dinner, put it on a small plate and leave it outside for the *nisse*. In the morning whatever remains of the food, bury in the earth. Make sure to record the whole ceremony in your journal and also record how some of these experiences made you feel.

The Morrigan, Celtic Goddess of War

The Morrigan is the Celtic goddess of sovereignty, magic, battle and fertility. She is a triple goddess often seen as a trio of goddesses consisting of Anu, Babd and Macha. She is daughter to the Earth Goddess Ernmas, and plays many roles throughout her complex myths.1 Her name translates to mean *"Great Queen"*, from the Gaelic word *moçr* which translates to *great*, and the second part of her name *rigan* meaning *queen*. 2

She is thought to have many different guises or faces as a goddess. The Morrigan can be the Crone or the Faery Queen. She can be the warrioress, earth mother, goddess of sovereignty and shape-shifter, among many others. After my research it seems as though The Morrigan has nine dominant faces. Which would seem to make her a nine-fold Goddess. Along with the fact of her being a triple goddess as well. The Morrigan exudes power over many domains, and was viewed as a very prominent figure in Celtic mythology.

Her most well known guise, is that of the goddess of war. In Celtic times it was not uncommon to have women fighting alongside men in battle. In fact it was quite common. 3 The war deities of the Celtic world were mostly female. The Morrigan was called on during war to grant the fighters victory in battle. Although she is a goddess of war and battle, this is not her most prominent role.

When men became kings of lands they had to marry the goddess that represented that land, and only she could grant sovereignty for the king to hold claim to the land. So the king was dedicated to his goddess and his land. The Morrigan was a goddess of sovereignty which made her more of a guardian or protector. 5 In the book *"The Concept of the Goddess"*, Maire Herbert writes that "She was not so much a war goddess, but more like a *protector* during war." People would call on her for their protection during battle and she would protect and guard those who called on her at any cost.

Being a goddess of sovereignty connects her to the land, and since she is also an earth goddess, this would connect her with the earth that much more. She was also a lover and sexual goddess linking her with fertility. In Ireland, in County Meath, there are two hills that are named *"The two breasts of Morrigan"*. So her source of fertility was portrayed through the earth, as the earth was seen as fertile, they connected this with The Morrigan as well. 6 As they did for other goddesses such as Anu, in *"The Paps of Anu"* in Killarney, Ireland.

We see The Morrigan in her guise as the lover in the battle of *Mag Tuired*, where she couples with The Dagda who is known as the *"Ruler of the Gods"* or *"The Good God"*. In the myth, The Dagda encounters The Morrigan washing in a river with one foot to the south of the river and the other to the north. They make love and then The Morrigan declares that she will offer assistance to his people in the upcoming battle. The place of this sexual encounter is said to be called *"The Bed of the couple"* in Irish Myth. 7

The Morrigan has many myths throughout the ancient Irish legends. Those that are her most famous are those dealing with the war hero Cu Chulainn. One day, The Morrigan appeared to Cu Chulainn and offered him her love. Although he didn't recognize her and he rejected her. The Morrigan became enraged at this and insulted him. He went to lash out at her but before he could, she turned into a crow and landed on a nearby tree. Realizing now who she was, Cu Chulainn said that had he known who she was before, he wouldn't have acted the way he did. But it was too late The Morrigan was angry and she gave Cu Chulainn a series of bad prophecies. One of those being that he would die in battle. She then declared to him that she would guard his death. 8 This is where her guise as goddess of sovereignty and war comes in. She is the protector and guardian over the land and its warriors.

Throughout the myths involving The Morrigan and Cu Chulainn, they seem to have an adversarial relationship. The myth of *"The Washer at the Ford"* takes place when Cu Chulainn was on his way to battle and he encounters a hag (The Morrigan) washing his bloody armor. This is seen as a bad omen. Later when the hero Cu Chulainn finally dies in battle, he ties himself to a standing stone and a crow lands on his shoulder. 9 This is The Morrigan guarding her dead warrior.

This wonderfully complex goddess was also connected to faeries, in her aspect as Queen of the Faeries. It is said in Irish myth that The Morrigan would lead her faery court across the land every Samhain night. She was also sometimes seen as the Banshee, which was a type of faery that would watch over a family and whose screeching cry foretold of a death within the family. 10 Being Queen of the faeries also connects her with mysticism and magic. She was indeed a goddess of prophecy and magic. Her famous battle cry would kill her warrior's enemies, her shape shifting abilities and her powerful uses of the elements were all part of her magic.

She was also known for divining and was known to be a seeress. 11 In her form as Morgan le Fay, Priestess of Avalon and sister to King Arthur, she was known as a sorceress. In some of the Arthurian myths, Morgan le Fay was portrayed as an evil practitioner of bad magic. In other myths she is seen as more of a priestess of the old ways. In her guise as Morgan le Fay, she is the witch and magical enchantress. 12

The Morrigan can appear to us in all of her forms, or only some. I believe a goddess will appear to you in the form you need most from her. Since The Morrigan has so many different faces and roles she plays throughout legend, it might be best to try and connect with all or as many as you can so you can get an idea of which of her guises works best with your energy. All of Celtic lore was passed down orally, so many of the myths might have been twisted in translation by later people who wrote them. The best way to truly understand a goddess, is to call on her energy and get to know her. In the following pages you will do exercises and a guided meditation to help you connect with this Goddess of War.

Goddess Connections

The Morrigan, in her many guises, has much wisdom to teach us. With her shape-shifting abilities, she shows us how to change at will and adapt easily to our environment. Sometimes throughout our lives we all experience some form of change, our lives can change all the time, and we have to be ready for it. The Morrigan teaches us to accept this change and learn to adapt quickly. This helps us to continue on with confidence and know that we are in control of the situation. She can also help us with divination, claiming our own inner sovereignty and our inner warrior woman. These next exercises will help you to connect with a few of the powerful faces of The Morrigan.

Guided Meditation to Meet The Morrigan

Guided meditation is an essential part of connecting with your goddess. Not only does it relax your body, it also prepares your mind to connect to her energy. In this exercise you will take a journey to meet The Morrigan and ask her for guidance for any issues that are troubling you.

Before any meditation make sure to ground and center yourself. Take some slow and deep breaths in and out a few times until you feel relaxed. You may also want to burn a smudge stick to cleanse the area. Once you feel centered you may start the meditation.

Imagine that you are walking along rolling hills of green, with hints of flowers here and there. The wind is blowing through your hair and it's an overcast day with a slight pink glow from the sunset. As you are walking along, you approach a small cave and you see light coming from within it so you enter. As you go in you notice a small fire with a woman standing behind it. As you get closer you notice the woman has long red hair and a long black dress, she makes eye contact with you and beckons you to her.

Once you're standing next to her she smiles at you and all of a sudden a crow comes flying in and lands on her shoulder. It is then that you realize that she is The Morrigan. You smile back at her and she holds out her hand for you to take it. You do, and she walks you over to the entrance of the cave. She asks you *"Are you ready for your journey of transformation?"* You say yes. She nods her head and the crow on her shoulder takes off into the sky. The Morrigan then changes form into that of a crow and takes flight. She looks back at you for you to do the same. You feel your body change, you are covered in black feathers and you're flying alongside The Morrigan. You both soar above the land for a while, looking down upon all the green beautiful hills and forests. (Take a moment to really take all this in, allow yourself to fly with her for a little while).

Now you notice that you are approaching an open field. The Morrigan looks at you and starts to soar back down to the land. Once she reaches the land, she transforms into a wolf. You fly down to the ground and do the same. Now you are running alongside the Morrigan as a wolf. You run through the field and back through the forest, hopping over rocks and branches with great agility and speed. The wind is blowing through your fur and you feel exhilarated. (Take a moment to really take all this in, allow yourself to run alongside her for a little while). Now you notice you are both reaching a cliff that juts out into the ocean, it has a small path down to the beach. The Morrigan trots down to the beach with you following behind. Once you reach the sand and you're both standing in front of the ocean, she looks back at you and then starts running towards the water.

Once she reaches the water's edge she slowly turns into an eel gliding through the water with ease. You also transform into an eel, gliding along beside her. You both swim through the ocean going deep and feeling the power of the water as you swim through it. (Take a moment to really take all this in, allow yourself to swim alongside her for a little while). The Morrigan then stops with you next to her and she tells you to stay still and close your eyes. She slowly wraps her eel body around yours until you are both intertwined with each other. You both start spinning and then all of a sudden, when you open your eyes, you realize you are back at the cave of

Cruachan. You thank The Morrigan for the amazing journey. She smiles at you and says *"Never forget the power of transformation "*. She then turns into a crow and flies away.

Now you get up and walk out of the cave of Cruachan, you walk back through the green rolling hills where you came from. Take a few deep breaths to come back. Once you feel ready, open your eyes and ground yourself. Take a few cleansing breaths and make sure to thank The Morrigan for her guidance. Leave a small offering of wine or honey.

Write down your experience in your journal. Your answer may not come to you right away, but soon enough it will reveal itself to you. If you feel the need, practice this meditation a few times until you get a more concrete answer.

The Morrigan's Ritual for Inner Strength

One of the strongest faces of The Morrigan is that of goddess of sovereignty. Meaning that she had complete and total power over the land and any man who became King, had to marry her. Then she would also grant him sovereignty over the land. Although they both held power over the land, The Morrigan held supreme power, and could strip the King of his if she thought he no longer deserved it.

Having inner sovereignty over ourselves means having complete and total power over ourselves. Mind, body and soul. To be powerful, to make our own decisions, and to be the rulers of our own lives.

Supplies:
Candle
Incense
Sage bundle
Offering of wine or dragon's blood resin

You can perform this ritual on the new moon or the full. Set up your altar with your candle, incense and sage. Light your sage bundle and cleanse your area and yourself with the smoke. Then light your candle and incense, take a few deep breaths in and out and center yourself. Recite:

Lady Morrigan, woman of power,
Lend me your strength at this bewitching hour,
Goddess of Sovereignty, ruler of kings
Help me to claim supreme sovereignty within me,
I wish for inner power, to be ruler of my life
Dark Goddess, Queen of the land,
Grant my wish on this new moon night!

Imagine your body filling with white light starting at the crown of your head and moving down through your body until it reaches your toes. Imagine that this light is filled with The Morrigan's power of strength. Hold this image for a few minutes and visualize yourself as being filled with inner strength. However that feels to you imagine it fully. Allow the strength and power of The Morrigan to flow through your body. After a few minutes imagine the white light leaving your body back through your crown. Even though the light is no longer there, the energy of inner strength is within you now. Meditate for a few minutes and ask The Morrigan if she has any messages for you. Thank The Morrigan and leave her an offering of wine or dragon's blood resin. Record everything in your journal.

Divination Ritual with The Morrigan

In this exercise you will be performing a ritual to call on The Morrigan's power of prophecy to help with your divination. We all use different methods of divination like runes, tarot cards, etc. Use whichever method you would normally use for this spell. In divination nothing is set in stone. If you perform a reading and you don't like the outcome it gave you, you always have the ability to change your path. If you don't normally use any kind of divination tool, you may want to purchase one for this exercise or get creative and make your own. This ritual is best performed on the new moon.

Supplies:
Divination tool (runes, cards, etc.)
Sage bundle
One candle
Offering of red wine

Set up your divination tools, light your candle and your smudge stick and cleanse the area, yourself and your tools with the smoke. Take a few deep breaths and ground and center yourself. Once you feel ready, recite:

I call on The Morrigan,
Mistress of Magick,
Lend me your sight,
On this, New Moon night,
Reveal to me what cannot be seen,
My path may be changed, but it's up to me.

Now perform your reading and be sure to write everything down in your journal including what your reading is telling you. Remember, just like it says in the invocation, your path can be changed but it's up to you. Or if you like the outcome of your reading, stay on your current path! After you're done clean everything up and leave an offering of red wine. Call on The Morrigan anytime you need her wisdom or assistance with a reading.

Brigid, Celtic Goddess of Poetry and Healing

Brigid is the Celtic goddess of poetry, creativity, smith-craft and healing. She is also associated with fire and water. The name Brigid in its Irish form means *"exalted"* and Brigid was referred to as *"The Exalted One"*. 1 Brigid is known as St. Bridget to the Christians who still honor her today. She is a very ancient and sacred goddess to the Celts and when Christianity threatened to take over their religious world they transformed Brigid into a saint so as to keep her followers as their own. Celtic myth and history has much mystery surrounding it as the Celts passed down their stories orally instead of writing them down. What we do know of the Celts mostly comes from what other cultures wrote of them so it is hard to decipher what is fact and what information was tainted by their enemies.

In some myths Brigid is the daughter of the Dagda or the "Good God" and in some she is his consort. 2 There is a creation myth involving these two gods and a sacred oak tree. In the beginning when the world was quite a great oak tree sprang forth from the fresh soil. From this sacred oak two acorns fell to the earth. From these acorns sprang the Dagda or "The Good God" and Brigid, "The Exalted One". The two gods looked upon their new world and decided to populate it with the children of Dana, the Mother Goddess. It is said that Brigid taught the children poetry, smith-craft and healing and the Dagda was known to them as the "Father of all Gods" 3

In some of the myths Dana and Brigid are seen as interchangeable. Brigid is also related to the Gallo-Roman goddess Brigantia. When the Romans invaded England they adopted some of their gods as their own, Brigid being one of them. 4 Celtic deities and myth were centered around the forces of nature and many of their gods were the literal representations of these. The Celtic gods were as fierce and primal as their people and were not known to be all-loving and gentle beings. I believe that many deities can be representative of how hard life is for a particular culture and for the ancient Celts life could be a harsh place. This was symbolized through their deities own stories, struggles and attributes.

Brigid is associated with water and sacred wells and as such there are many wells throughout Ireland which are sacred to Brigid. Some of these wells are located next to churches which were built after the wells and some are tucked away in the forests, hills and groves. 5 I had the pleasure of visiting a sacred well of Brigid in County Clare, Ireland. In front stands a statue of St. Bridget enclosed in a glass case with bushes and flowers all around. Behind her and down a dark cave-like passage lies the well. All along the walls are prayers written on paper, pictures and votive offerings asking Brigid for her healing blessings. In the well itself were coins which invoked a wish to be granted. Tied to the trees around the site were *clootie's* which are pieces of cloth that are dipped into the sacred wells and then tied to the trees. These are left to honor the deities or spirits associated with the sacred well.

This is just one of the many wells associated with Brigid throughout Ireland. As Brigid is associated with water, she is also associated with fire. Brigid has an association with the sun and has been depicted with a flaming sun crown upon her head. This may be where her association with fire comes from. In the village of Kildare there lies a shrine to Brigid which houses an eternal flame in her honor. The site which is now a church is thought to have once been a pagan shrine with nineteen priestesses or druidesses who tended the eternal flame. The number nineteen is thought to come from the nineteen-year cycle of the Celtic "great year". Each night a priestess tends the flame of Brigid and one the twentieth night the goddess tends the flame herself. This tradition was then practiced later by the Christian nuns in the church of Brigid. 6

Brigid's most well-known holiday is Imbolc which is celebrated on February 1. This day marks the beginning of spring for the Celts. It is a time of rebirth and fertility. Imbolc was a major holiday for the Celts and as such there are many recorded Imbolc traditions. One of these involved what's known as a *Brideog* in which families would construct a doll made out of rushes and reeds. They would dress the doll to appear as a young girl and then bring the doll from house to house. This was seen to be a blessing from Brigid on the whole community. 7

Imbolc was a time when the first new shoots of green would sprout up from the snow. It was a time of hope after surviving a harsh winter. It was a time of fertility for the animals as well as for the people. Brigid was associated with cows and their life sustaining milk which was also honored at Imbolc. Cows and their milk were said to represent the sacred nature of motherhood. 8 It is said that many births took place around Imbolc. This was so that the women could rest during the winter when not much work was to be done and give birth in the spring. 9

Brigid was seen as the giver of life at Imbolc and the promise of Spring. Imbolc was also a fire festival and was one of the four big fire festivals of the Celtic year. As such when Brigid was turned into St. Bridget by the Christians, a holiday known as Candlemas came into being which takes place on February 2nd. During this holiday churches are known to light many candles and will sometimes host candlelit processions. This mimics the great fires of Imbolc from earlier pagan times.

Brigid is also a goddess of bards, poetry and the creative arts. Since the Celts passed down their stories orally the Bard became an integral part of the community. Music was very important to the ancient Celts and as such the Bards would sing their stories while playing an instrument. The Bards were also said to work with the Druids and took part in religious ceremonies. 10 All of this was seen as sacred to Brigid and music and poetry were seen as her gifts. Because of this Brigid can be seen as a goddess of inspiration and can be called upon for any creative needs.

In the following pages you will do exercises and a guided meditation to help you connect with this Goddess of inspiration.

Goddess Connections

Brigid was and is still deeply loved and revered by her followers. She represents the eternal flame which burns inside all of us. The flame of passion which propels us into following our dreams and creating the life we truly want. Brigid is associated with Spring and as such she represents rebirth and renewal. The promise of new life and new beginnings. She gives us hope during the cold and dark points in our lives much like the cold and dark nights of Winter. Brigid also helps us with creativity and shows us how to ignite our creative spark.

Guided Meditation to Meet Brigid

Guided meditation is an essential part of connecting with your goddess. Not only does it relax your body, it also prepares your mind to connect to her energy. In this exercise you will take a journey to meet Brigid, and ask her for guidance for any issues that are troubling you. Before any meditation make sure to ground and center yourself. Take some slow and deep breaths in and out a few times until you feel relaxed. You may also want to burn a smudge stick to cleanse the area. Once you feel centered you may start the meditation.

Imagine that you are walking on emerald green hills that stretch on for miles. You are standing on the top of one hill and you close your eyes to feel the breeze against your skin. You hear something that sounds like water but you don't see any rivers or streams. As you start to look around for its source you notice a small stone staircase on the side of the hill which winds down and around the hill you're standing on. You follow the staircase and as it winds down you notice that it leads to a small underground alcove. You enter the alcove and a few feet in front of you there is a hole in the ground filled with water. There are Brigid's crosses and votive offerings all around and you realize that this is a sacred well for Brigid.

There is an ancient and sacred energy here. You sit down in front of the well and close your eyes to better feel and connect to the energy. Sit there for a minute and feel the energy around you. Absorb it in your soul and become one with your surroundings. When you open your eyes again there is a beautiful pale skinned woman with flaming red hair standing before you in the well. She has a small Brigid's cross around her neck and she is holding a tall staff. You realize that this is the goddess Brigid. You stand to greet her and she smiles as she embraces you in a warm hug. You thank her for showing herself to you and honoring you with her presence.

She tells you that this is her sacred well which has ancient healing properties. She tells you that in order to heal yourself you must cleanse yourself in her well. She tells you to sit down in front of the well and place your hands over the water. She then kneels down next to you and places her hands over yours. She imparts her healing energy through your hands and into the well. You watch as both your hands glow with a warm white light which flows down into the water. When she is done, she instructs you to grab some of the water with cupped hands and pour it over your head. She tells you to do this three times. You do as she says and when the water falls over your head it feels warm and energized. You immediately feel a little lighter and alive. Feel the water falling down your head and over your face. Feel the droplets falling off you face and back into the well.

You pour the water over your head three times and each time you feel more revitalized and refreshed. When you are done cleansing yourself with the water Brigid instructs you to stand up and thank the well for its curative properties. You thank the well and then you turn to her and thank her also. She embraces you in another warm hug and tells you that anytime you need to heal yourself you may come to her well. She then walks back over to the well, steps inside and disappears in a foggy mist back into the well.

You then walk out of the alcove and slowly start to walk back up the stone stairs. Once you reach the top you walk back to the top of the hill. Take a few deep breaths to come back. Once you feel ready, open your eyes and ground yourself. Take a few cleansing breaths and make sure to thank Brigid for her guidance.

Write down your experience in your journal. Your answer may not come to you right away, but soon enough it will reveal itself to you. If you feel the need, practice this meditation a few times until you get a more concrete answer.

Brigid's Fires of Inspiration Charm

Brigid is a goddess of poetry and inspiration. She is known to spark creativity and inspire the muse within ourselves. In this ritual you will use her two elements of fire and water in order to inspire your inner creative spirit. Since Brigid is also a healing goddess and is associated with water and wells you will use water to heal yourself with a warm bath before you begin the ritual.

Supplies:
Epsom salts
Three tea-light candles
Sage bundle
Incense
Offering of wine

Fill up your tub with warm water and a cup of Epsom salts. You may also wish to add some lavender essential oil if you have it. Stir up your bath so the salt dissolves and ask Brigid to imbue the water with her powers of healing. Now proceed with your bath taking as long as you need to soak and fully relax. Once you're done prepare for your ritual. Set up your altar with your three tea-lights sitting in a row, the number three is sacred to the Celts and Brigid is known as a three-fold goddess so your three candles represent this. Place your incense and your offering on your altar and light your sage bundle. Cleanse yourself and your area with the smoke and then light your candles and incense. Recite:

Brigid, Lady of Fire

Light the creative spark within me
Ignite that passionate fire in my soul
Inspire my inner muse
I wish for the flames of inspiration to burn within me
So that I may be inspired to create
As I will it, so shall it be

Meditate for a few minutes and imagine a bright flame burning within your heart. Hold this image for a little while. Visualize yourself creating something new and inspired. Imagine how it would feel during and after you've been inspired to create. Meditate for a few more minutes and once you feel ready slowly start to come out of your meditation. Thank Brigid and leave your offering for her. Record everything in your journal and take note of any new inspirations over the following days.

<u>Make a Brigid's Cross</u>

A Brigid's cross was usually made around the time of Imbolc which is Brigid's sacred day. They can be made with many different materials but the most common used are reeds, rush, and wheat. You can find any of these things at your local craft or grocery stores. Once you have completed making your cross you will ask Brigid to bless it and then you can hang it anywhere in your house or keep it on your altar.

Supplies:
28-inch-long wheat straws, reeds, whatever you will be using
Twine for securing the ends
One candle
Sage bundle
Incense
Offering of white flowers

First you will need to soak your reeds in a large container of water for about an hour before you can construct the cross. While they're soaking set up your altar with your candle, incense and offering. Once the reeds are ready take them to your altar to make the cross. Light your sage bundle and cleanse yourself, your area and the reeds. Light the candle and incense and recite:

Brigid, Lady of Creation
Guide me in creating this cross in your honor
May it be blessed with your healing energy and light

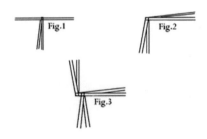

Now start to make your cross. Follow the diagram above. First create the middle by positioning two straws to make a plus sign placing the horizontal reed on top. Pull the vertical reed down on top of its other half (Fig 1). Turn the reed 90 degrees counterclockwise. Repeat to fold down the reed that is now vertical (Fig 2) Turn the reeds 90 degrees counterclockwise again to add the next reed. Place it to the right of the vertically folded reed and under the horizontal one (Fig 3).

Fold the reed, turn the reeds again and add the fourth reed in the same way. Repeat this process with the rest of the straws while trying to not let them bunch up in the middle. Try to lay them side by side and build the cross outwards. It might bunch up a little at first but once the cross starts coming together you'll be able to see which areas need adjusting. Try also not to make it too tight so you do have room for correcting errors.

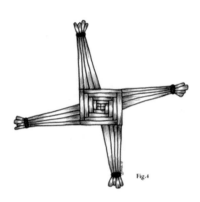

Fig.4

When your cross is complete, tie off each end with some twine, ribbon or anything else you'd like. Tie the ends an inch or two in from the actual end (Fig 4). Now that your cross is finished, pass it through some sage smoke and ask Brigid to bless it for you. Keep it on your altar or hang it somewhere in your home to receive the blessings of Brigid.

Yemaya, Yoruban Mother Goddess of the Ocean

Yemaya, is the Yoruban goddess of the oceans and rivers and is known as a mother goddess. She is also known as a goddess of creation and rebirth. Her worship originated in the Yoruban region of Nigeria, Africa and spread to islands like Cuba and the Bahamas as well as Brazil. The Yoruban deities, which are known as Orisha's within the African/Santerian tradition, each have their own myth, just like in any other culture. The word for myth in the Yoruban culture was *pataki* and each Orisha has their own *pataki*.

In order to truly understand this goddess learning about where she originated from is very important. Since her worship has spread far and wide her image has changed a little from culture to culture. 1 The Yoruban religion was one that was shrouded in mysticism and connection with the divine, or the Orisha's. Archaeologists have proven that the Yoruban area of Nigeria has been inhabited for over forty thousand years so the exact time the Yoruban religion began is unknown. It is said to be quite an old spiritual belief. 2

When the slave trade began around the 1500's, Yoruban people were sent to the America's to be used as slaves, and they took their religion with them. Being that the act of slavery was a horrible time in America, this was also the reason for the spread of the Yoruban religious concepts and deities to parts of the islands, and the America's. 3 Divination was an essential aspect of the Yoruban religion. Their method of divination was called *diloggun* and they used what was known as *odu* for their divining. There are sixteen total *odu*, and basically what each of these represent are different stories and symbols of Yoruban wisdom and teachings. Each is represented by a cowrie shell which has the smooth part of the shell cut off so they do not all look the same. This helps with the divination process. The stories behind each *odu* are very complex and meaningful.4

There is a tale about Yemaya and how she longed to learn *diloggun*.

Yemaya's husband Orunmila was the greatest diviner and people came from all over to see him. Yemaya had taken an interest in the *odu* and decided to learn herself. Although being that she is Orunmila's wife, she was not allowed to learn the *diloggun*, and he does not want her to learn it. She decides to secretly listen and watch her husband when he gives his readings so she may learn. She picks up the art of divining with the cowrie shells rather quickly. Soon after, Yemaya started seeing clients when her husband would leave town for a period of time.

Orunmila started noticing that he and his wife seemed to have more money and were doing very well. He immediately became suspicious of Yemaya. The next time he tells Yemaya he is going out of town for a bit, he comes back disguised. When he arrives home he notices lots of people standing in line in front of his house. He asks why there are so many people here and they tell him they are here to see Yemaya the diviner! Orunmila becomes enraged and gets in line to wait to see his wife. When it's finally his turn he approaches Yemaya and when she realizes that this man is her husband, she becomes filled with fear.

Orunmila tells Yemaya that only one diviner is allowed to live under his roof but Yemaya loves the *odu* so much that she won't give it up. Orunmila is so upset that Yemaya will not give up divining that he vows to never again use the *odu*. 5 There are different versions of this *pataki* in which Oshun, Yemaya's sister, was Orunmila's wife first before Yemaya.

The Yoruban people revered nature in all of her aspects, and many of their Orisha's represent these natural elements. Yemaya, being Mother of the Oceans, was also known as *"The Mother of All"*. She is portrayed as a sensitive and compassionate mother figure called upon for childbirth, comfort, healing and rebirth. She is seen as the greatest deity on the Yoruban pantheon. Even more so than her father Obatala, a Father God who was seen as the creator of mankind. Believing that all life comes from the water, Yemaya is seen as the creator of the earth itself, and all of her creatures. In Santeria she is known as *Iya Moaye* or *Mother of the World.* 6

She was known to cure infertility and help women with childbirth. She was also seen as being very motherly and protective. It is said that Yemaya was married to several of the Orisha, and also had love affairs with some of them. Since her worship spread from Africa, she took on different forms in other areas. In Voodoo magic she is seen as a moon goddess. In Brazil and the Caribbean she is viewed as the Great Mother of the Oceans. 7 Just as a mother can be protective and loving, they can also be fierce, as is Yemaya. She can also be invoked for prosperity and can help you create abundance in your own life.

There are festivals throughout the year which take place in honor of Yemaya still to this day. One of those is on February 2, on which Yemaya is honored as *She Whose Children are Fish*". It is celebrated on the beaches of Brazil and other South American countries. For this feast women wear all white and enter the sea barefoot with offerings of flowers, jewelry and shells amongst other things for Yemaya. They have a feast which consists of her favorite food while music plays and dancing ensues. They then set boats to sail which carry offerings and prayers that are to be delivered into Yemaya's element. 8

Yemaya is also honored on New Year's Eve in Brazil. For this celebration people gather at the beach to give offerings to Yemaya. Her devotees, dressed in all white, throw white flowers into the ocean in the hopes that Yemaya will grant them wishes. They also give floating lit candles and tiny boats filled with offerings to the Mother of the Oceans.

Yemaya has much to teach us as she is full of ancient and primal knowledge. In the following pages you will do exercises and a guided meditation to help you connect with this Mother Goddess of Oceans.

Goddess Connections

Yemaya is the Mother of Oceans and as such she represents the ebb and flow of the ever-changing tides. Like the water, she can be life-giving and tranquil. Water can also be a destructive force to deal with and as it can create life, it can also take it away. Yemaya teaches us to go with the flow of life and it's ever-changing attributes just like the ocean. She also helps us with rebirth and creating the life we want. Yemaya tells us that in order to be reborn we must first be transformed which is not usually an easy process.

Guided Meditation to meet Yemaya

In this guided meditation you will go on a journey with Yemaya in her own element, the water. This meditation is good to practice for healing and to help you learn how to move through life a little easier, to flow with the ups and downs, just like the waves of the vast ocean.

Before any meditation make sure to ground and center yourself. Take some slow and deep breaths in and out a few times until you feel relaxed. You may also want to burn a smudge stick to cleanse the area. Once you feel centered you may start the meditation.

Imagine you are walking down a sandy path to the beach surrounded by sea grass. Feel the warm sand beneath your feet and the cool breeze in the air coming from the ocean. As you reach the end of the path, you see the vast expanse of the ocean and the long sandy beach before your eyes. It is just before sunrise so you sit down on the sand to watch and savor the beauty. As the sun starts to rise you stare in awe at how amazing and entrancing the beauty of it is. You close your eyes as the sun gets brighter and rises higher and when you open them, you see a beautiful woman standing before you.

She has gorgeous dark hair and dark eyes, and is wearing a beautiful white silky dress and jewelry made of shells and pearls. She smiles at you while you get to your feet. You realize that this woman before you is Yemaya of the oceans, Great Mother of All. You greet her and thank her for coming to you. She hugs you with a motherly embrace. She says to you *"Why don't you come with me to my world for a little journey?"*. She takes your hand and leads you to the water, you enter the ocean and it feels cool against your skin. She takes you under the waves as you hold hands and flow along with the water. All of a sudden Yemaya turns into a beautiful bronze skinned mermaid, with shiny scales of pearly white and aqua blue.

She swims with you faster still holding your hand and you begin to feel the force and power of the water. All around you are sea turtles, fish, porpoises among many other sea creatures swimming along with you. The dolphins play with you and swim between you both while making sweet noises that almost sound like giggles. You realize how much fun you're having and how much positive love Yemaya and all the beautiful creatures around you are bringing to you.

After a little longer of swimming and enjoying your time with this Great Goddess and all her creatures, Yemaya stops. She says to you *"My child, sometimes you have to learn to flow with life just as the water flows. You must learn to live in the moment and let the flow of life take you to where you need to be, and remember to have fun along the way!"*. You thank Yemaya for her wisdom and for the opportunity to enter and become one with her realm.

She then takes you back to shore. When you both get out of the water, Yemaya morphs back into her goddess form. She hugs you close and deep like a mothers loving embrace. You feel her loving energy running through you, and that helps you to feel comfort and happiness. After your embrace, she turns back towards the water and disappears under the waves. Now you walk back towards the sandy path with the sea grass. Take a few deep breaths to come back. Once you feel ready, open your eyes and ground yourself. Take a few cleansing breaths and make sure to thank Yemaya for her guidance

Write down your experience in your journal. Your answer may not come to you right away but soon enough it will reveal itself to you. If you feel the need, practice this meditation a few times until you get a more concrete answer.

Creation and Rebirth Ritual with Yemaya

Since Yemaya is a goddess of all creation, she can be called upon to inspire creation and rebirth in your own life. Whatever it may be, a creative venture, a new life, or maybe a new career, Yemaya can help you to produce this for yourself. This spell should be performed on the full moon.

Supplies:
Piece of paper
Fire proof dish/cauldron
Sage bundle
Offerings of cowrie shells, white flowers or white wine

Cleanse your area and yourself with the sage. Now set up your altar and write on your piece of paper what it is your trying to create, while visualizing your desire/goal. Visualize it happening, and visualize it after it's happened as well. Now light your candle and incense and invoke Yemaya.

Recite:
Yemaya, ancient Mother of water and life,
Help me to create my desires on this full moon night,
With your healing waters of creation,
Cleanse myself to be reborn,
And prepare my body to give birth to my new world.
Comfort my soul along the way
With your compassionate motherly ocean waves.

Now burn your paper with your desire written on it, and visualize the smoke taking your wish out to the universe. Meditate and visualize for a few minutes about your new life and how it will be once you have achieved your goal. Let the candle burn down completely, and leave your offerings. If you live near water of some kind, like a lake or the ocean, or any body of water, throw the ashes from your paper into it, since this is Yemaya's element, it will flow easily to her. Make sure to record everything down in your journal.

Making a Sacred Eleke for Yemaya

Elekes are beaded necklaces that correspond by color to each Orisha. These are given to initiates of the Santerian tradition. Yemaya's colors are white and blue these will be the color beads to use when crafting her devotional necklace. Feel free to use any type of bead for this necklace such as seed beads, crystals, pony beads etc. You can choose any design for the beads. Either alternating white and blue, seven (Yemaya's sacred number) white and seven blue alternating, or any kind of bead combination that you find pleasing.

Supplies:
White and blue beads
Jewelry thread/elastic thread
Sage bundle
Simple shrine in honor of Yemaya

Set up a simple shrine to Yemaya with colors of white and blue, a candle and a seashell. Gather your beads and thread for your necklace and cleanse the area with your sage. To make your necklace, measure it for how long you would like it and make sure to leave a few extra inches on each end for when you complete it. I made an eleke and I chose to make it 24 inches long. Before you start recite this prayer to Yemaya:

Yemaya, Mother of the blue oceans
Guide me in making a sacred eleke in your honor

Take your string and tie a knot on one end. String all your beads on your thread in whichever pattern you choose. When you've finished putting all of your beads on the string, take the two end pieces of string and tie them together about three times. Make sure your knot is tight, but no so tight that it breaks. Now your eleke is finished and its time to cleanse it. Ask Yemaya to bless your eleke with her energies. You may also wish to bless it in the ocean or a body of water, or simply purify it with sage or incense smoke. Now your eleke is ready to wear! You may choose to wear it only during ritual or at any time you wish.

Sources

Isis

1. Patricia Monaghan, *The Goddess Path, Myths, Invocations & Rituals,* (Llewellyn, 1999) 161

2. R.E. Witt, *Isis in the Ancient World,* (John Hopkins University Press, 1971) 37 - 40

3. DeTraci Regula, *The Mysteries of Isis, Her Worship and Magick*, (Llewellyn Publications, 1995) 115-117

4. R.E. Witt, *Isis in the Ancient World,* (John Hopkins University Press, 1971) 186

5. R.E. Witt, *Isis in the Ancient World,* (John Hopkins University Press, 1971) 166

6. Patricia Monaghan, *The Goddess Path, Myths, Invocations & Rituals,* (Llewellyn, 1999) 164

7. DeTraci Regula, *The Mysteries of Isis, Her Worship and Magick*, (Llewellyn Publications, 1995)104-112

8. DeTraci Regula, *The Mysteries of Isis, Her Worship and Magick*, (Llewellyn Publications, 1995) 142-143,

9. DeTraci Regula, *The Mysteries of Isis, Her Worship and Magick*, (Llewellyn Publications, 1995) 137

10. R.E. Witt, *Isis in the Ancient World,* (John Hopkins University Press, 1971) 141 - 151

11. R.E. Witt, *Isis in the Ancient World,* (John Hopkins University Press, 1971) 44

12. R.E. Witt, *Isis in the Ancient World,* (John Hopkins University Press, 1971) 34

Hathor

1.Lesley Jackson, *Hathor a Reintroduction to an Ancient Egyptian Goddess,* (Avalonia, 2014) 129

2.Alison Roberts, *Hathor Rising, The Power of the Goddess in Ancient Egypt*, (Inner Traditions International, 1997) 9

3.Lesley Jackson, *Hathor a Reintroduction to an Ancient Egyptian Goddess,* (Avalonia, 2014) 463

4.Lesley Jackson, *Hathor a Reintroduction to an Ancient Egyptian Goddess,* (Avalonia, 2014) 527

5.Patricia Monaghan, *The Goddess Path, Myths, Invocations & Rituals,* (Llewellyn, 1999) 81

6.Lesley Jackson, *Hathor a Reintroduction to an Ancient Egyptian Goddess,* (Avalonia, 2014) 76

7.Lesley Jackson, *Hathor a Reintroduction to an Ancient Egyptian Goddess,* (Avalonia,

2014) 361

8. Lesley Jackson, *Hathor a Reintroduction to an Ancient Egyptian Goddess,* (Avalonia, 2014) 401

9. Alison Roberts, *Hathor Rising, The Power of the Goddess in Ancient Egypt*, (Inner Traditions International, 1997) 9

10. Alison Roberts, *Hathor Rising, The Power of the Goddess in Ancient Egypt*, (Inner Traditions International, 1997) 11

11. Carolyn Graves-Brown, *Dancing for Hathor, Women in Ancient Egypt,* (Continuum UK, 2010) 96

12. Alison Roberts, *Hathor Rising, The Power of the Goddess in Ancient Egypt*, (Inner Traditions International, 1997) 14

13. Lesley Jackson, *Hathor a Reintroduction to an Ancient Egyptian Goddess,* (Avalonia, 2014) 401

14. Alison Roberts, *Hathor Rising, The Power of the Goddess in Ancient Egypt*, (Inner Traditions International, 1997) 13

15. Lesley Jackson, *Hathor a Reintroduction to an Ancient Egyptian Goddess,* (Avalonia, 2014) pg 1650

16. Carolyn Graves-Brown, *Dancing for Hathor, Women in Ancient Egypt,* (Continuum UK, 2010) 90

17. Lesley Jackson, *Hathor a Reintroduction to an Ancient Egyptian Goddess,* (Avalonia, 2014) 1707

18. Lesley Jackson, *Hathor a Reintroduction to an Ancient Egyptian Goddess,* (Avalonia, 2014) 1879

19. Ibid

Aphrodite

1. Paul Friedrich, *The Meaning of Aphrodite*, (University of Chicago Press, 1978) 11-12

2. Nancy Qualls-Corbett, *The Sacred Prostitute, Eternal Aspect of the Feminine,* (Inner City Books 1988) 57-58

3. Paul Friedrich, *The Meaning of Aphrodite*, (University of Chicago Press, 1978)13-14

4. Nancy Qualls-Corbett, *The Sacred Prostitute, Eternal Aspect of the Feminine,* (Inner City Books 1988) 55

5. Paul Friedrich, *The Meaning of Aphrodite*, (University of Chicago Press, 1978) 18-19

6. Patricia Monaghan, The *Goddess Path,* (Llewellyn Publications, 1999) 93 – 94

7. Laurelei Black, *Aphrodite's Priestesses,* (CreateSpace Independent, 2009) 22-23

8. Laurelei Black, *The Cult of Aphrodite,* (CreateSpace Independent, 2010) 84

9. Rachel Rosenzweig, *Worshiping Aphrodite, Art and Cult in Classical Athens*, (University of Michigan Press, 2004) 16

10. Ibid

11. Laurelei Black, *The Cult of Aphrodite,* (CreateSpace Independent, 2010) 47

12. Laurelei Black, *The Cult of Aphrodite,* (CreateSpace Independent, 2010) 64
13. Laurelei Black, *The Cult of Aphrodite,* (CreateSpace Independent, 2010) 96

Hekate

1. Stephen Ronan, *The Goddess Hekate*, (Chthonios Books, 1992) 11-13
2. Sarah Isles Johnston, *Hekate Soteira,* (The American Philological Association, 1990) 21-22
3. Sorita d'Este, *Hekate Keys to the Crossroads,* (Avalonia, 2006) 20-23
4. Sorita d'Este & David Rankine, *Hekate Liminal Rites,* (Avalonia 2009) 137
5. Sorita d'Este & David Rankine, *Hekate Liminal Rites,* (Avalonia 2009) 126
6. Ibid
7. Stephen Ronan, *The Goddess Hekate,* (Chthonios Books, 1992) 57
8. Sorita d'Este, *Hekate, Her Sacred Fires*, (Avalonia, 2010) 35-36
9. Sorita d'Este & David Rankine, *Hekate Liminal Rites,* (Avalonia 2009)
10 Sarah Isles Johnston, *Hekate Soteira,* (The American Philological Association, 1990) 24

Artemis

1. Sorita D'Este, *Artemis, Virgin Goddess of the Sun, Moon & Hunt,* (Avalonia, 2005) 137
2. Agape Kyros, *Greek Mythology, Origins of Greek Mythology and the Twelve Olympian Gods,* (Boss Publishing, 2014) 216
3. Sorita D'Este, *Artemis, Virgin Goddess of the Sun, Moon & Hunt,* (Avalonia, 2005) 179
4. Agape Kyros, *Greek Mythology, Origins of Greek Mythology and the Twelve Olympian Gods,* (Boss Publishing, 2014) 216
5. Ibid
6. Patricia Monaghan, *The Goddess Path, Myths, Invocations & Rituals,* (Llewellyn, 1999) 127
7. Sorita D'Este, *Artemis, Virgin Goddess of the Sun, Moon & Hunt,* (Avalonia, 2005) 736
8. Sorita D'Este, *Artemis, Virgin Goddess of the Sun, Moon & Hunt,* (Avalonia, 2005) 772
9. R.E. Witt, *Isis in the Ancient World,* (John Hopkins University Press, 1971) 19
10. Sorita D'Este, *Artemis, Virgin Goddess of the Sun, Moon & Hunt,* (Avalonia, 2005)574
11. Sorita D'Este, *Artemis, Virgin Goddess of the Sun, Moon & Hunt,* (Avalonia, 2005) 640
12. Patricia Monaghan, *The Goddess Path, Myths, Invocations & Rituals,* (Llewellyn, 1999) 129

Freyja

1. Kevin Crossley-Holland, *The Norse Myths*, (Pantheon Books, 1980) 7 - 8

2. Kevin Crossley-Holland, *The Norse Myths*, (Pantheon Books, 1980) 65 - 69

3. Kevin Crossley-Holland, *The Norse Myths*, (Pantheon Books, 1980) Intro.

4. Kevin Crossley-Holland, *The Norse Myths*, (Pantheon Books, 1980) 100 - 103

5. Patricia Lafayllve, *Freyja, Lady Vanadis*, (Outskirts Press, 2006) 33- 34

6. Katie Gerrard, *Seidr The Gate Is Open*, (Avalonia, 2011) 31-49

7. Patricia Lafayllve, *Freyja, Lady Vanadis,* (Outskirts Press, 2006) 30

8. Patricia Lafayllve, *Freyja, Lady Vanadis,* (Outskirts Press, 2006) 1

9. Alice Karlsdottir, *Magic of the Norse Goddesses, Mythology, Ritual, Tranceworking,* (Runa-Raven Press, 2003) 169

The Morrigan

1. Stephanie Woodfield, *Celtic Lore & Spellcraft of the Dark Goddess,* (Llewellyn, 2011) 9

2. Sandra Billington & Miranda Green, *The Concept of the Goddess,* (Routledge, 1998) 142

3. David Rankine & Sorita D'Este, *The Guises of The Morrigan* (Avalonia, 2005) 50

4. Stephanie Woodfield, *Celtic Lore & Spellcraft of the Dark Goddess,* (Llewellyn, 2011) 35 – 37

5. Stephanie Woodfield, *Celtic Lore & Spellcraft of the Dark Goddess,* (Llewellyn, 2011) 198

6. Sandra Billington & Miranda Green, *The Concept of the Goddess,* (Routledge, 1998) 143

7. Sandra Billington & Miranda Green, *The Concept of the Goddess,* (Routledge, 1998) 142 - 143

8. Morgan Daimler, *Pagan Portals, The Morrigan, Meeting the Great Queens,* (Moon Books, 2014) 47

9. David Rankine & Sorita D'Este, *The Guises of The Morrigan* (Avalonia, 2005) 65 - 66

10. Stephanie Woodfield, *Celtic Lore & Spellcraft of the Dark Goddess,* (Llewellyn, 2011) 215 - 217

11. Stephanie Woodfield, *Celtic Lore & Spellcraft of the Dark Goddess,* (Llewellyn, 2011) 288 – 290

12. Ibid

Brigid

1. Mary Condren, *The Serpent and the Goddess,* (HarperCollins Publishers, 1989) 57

2.Ibid

3. Courtney Weber, *Brigid, History, Mystery and Magick of the Celtic Goddess* (Weiser Books, 2015) 336

4. T.W. Rolliston, *Myths and Legends of the Celtic Race,* (Constable & Company Limited, London, 1911) 1141

5.Courtney Weber, *Brigid, History, Mystery and Magick of the Celtic Goddess* (Weiser

Books, 2015) 512

6.Courtney Weber, *Brigid, History, Mystery and Magick of the Celtic Goddess* (Weiser Books, 2015) 1031

7.Courtney Weber, *Brigid, History, Mystery and Magick of the Celtic Goddess* (Weiser Books, 2015) 1916

8. Mary Condren, *The Serpent and the Goddess,* (HarperCollins Publishers, 1989) 58

9.Courtney Weber, *Brigid, History, Mystery and Magick of the Celtic Goddess* (Weiser Books, 2015) 1946

10. Mary Condren, *The Serpent and the Goddess,* (HarperCollins Publishers, 1989)57

Yemaya

1. Baba Ifa Karade, *Handbook of Yoruba Religious Concepts*, (Samuel Weiser, 1994) 1

2. Baba Ifa Karade, *Handbook of Yoruba Religious Concepts*, (Samuel Weiser, 1994) 2

3. Baba Ifa Karade, *Handbook of Yoruba Religious Concepts*, (Samuel Weiser, 1994) 3-4

4. Baba Ifa Karade, *Handbook of Yoruba Religious Concepts*, (Samuel Weiser, 1994) 11-13

5. Baba Raul Canizares, Yemaya, *Santeria and the Queen of the Seven Seas*, (Original Publications, 2006) 8-11

6. Migene Gonzalez-Wippler, *Powers of the Orishas, Santeria and the Worship of Saints* (Original Publications, 1992) 100

7. Migene Gonzalez Wippler, *Santeria: The Religion, Faith, Rites and Magic,* (Llewellyn, 2002) 57-59

8. Kim Huggens, *From a Drop of Water,* (Avalonia, 2009)106

Made in United States
Troutdale, OR
08/01/2023

11739405R00057